Th

D1587349

05328286

SIMPLY

SABRINA GHAYOUR

Darling Mathew — my brother, chief taster, wise teacher and much more — food always tastes so much better with you at our table.

SIMPLY
SABRINA GHAYOUR

EASY EVERYDAY DISHES
FROM THE BESTSELLING AUTHOR OF
Persiana

MITCHELL BEAZLEY

An Hachette UK Company
www.hachette.co.uk

First published in Great Britain in 2020 by Mitchell Beazley,
an imprint of Octopus Publishing Group Ltd
Carmelite House
50 Victoria Embankment
London EC4Y 0DZ
www.octopusbooks.co.uk

ISBN 978 1 78472 516 7

A CIP catalogue record for this book is available from
the British Library.

Printed and bound in China

10 9 8 7 6 5 4 3 2 1

Publishing Director: Stephanie Jackson
Senior Managing Editor: Sybella Stephens
Copy Editor: Jo Richardson
Senior Designer: Jaz Bahra
Photographer: Kris Kirkham
Food Stylist: Laura Field
Props Stylist: Agathe Gits
Senior Production Manager: Peter Hunt

Publisher's notes
Vegetarians should look for the 'V' symbol on cheese
to ensure it is made with vegetarian rennet.

Eggs should be medium unless otherwise stated. This
book contains dishes made with raw or lightly cooked
eggs. It is prudent for more vulnerable people such as
pregnant and nursing mothers, the elderly, babies and
young children to avoid uncooked or lightly cooked
dishes made with eggs.

Contents

Introduction

Being an only child whose parents didn't cook meant that I grew up unafraid to experiment, to break rules, to deviate from tradition and, at times, to fail miserably and start over. It was quite a galvanizing experience because, as you grow up, you cook without seeing obstacles or limitations and follow your gut and palate instincts about what feels good. More often than not it ends up tasting good, too.

I look back at all that I've learned in my food career and I realize that, perhaps as with you, I have evolved and improved in technique, gained more confidence in what may once have been obscure to me and am now so comfortable in my simple approach that, while I'll always be firmly rooted in the flavours of Iran and the Middle East, it's impossible to stick a specific label on my approach. It's just… Simply Sabrina.

As well as becoming at ease with blending together flavours of my heritage and those of my Western upbringing, my thirst for knowledge and curiosity about the food and flavours of other regions and cultures of the world have also enriched my cooking so much. My travels have introduced me to ingredients not typical of the Middle East that I now use to bolster flavour, create depth and, most importantly, provide satisfaction in every mouthful.

I wish I could tell you that I have cultivated some kind of solid structure in the way that I research my recipes, but the truth is, I haven't. As I cook, eat and learn, I simplify, create and pass on to you, having tested (and tested and tested) each recipe to produce the most simple and effective results. In my normal everyday life, I cook every single day – even on holiday. I usually can't stand to be away from the kitchen for more than a few days, which means I always choose apartments instead of hotels so that I can carry on cooking, tasting and constantly coming up with new ideas and inspiration to use at home. The majority of what makes the cut in my domestic culinary repertoire and shines as a clear favourite is what eventually makes it into my cookery classes and, in turn, into my books.

This book features a selection of my favourite authentic Persian recipes from my childhood, including some long-forgotten dishes that have been brought back to life by my loved ones asking me to try and recreate them. Translating the ingredients, methods and 'you have to do it this way'-isms into simplified, accessible recipes is the challenging part because every culture that reveres its culinary traditions will swear that you 'must only use this' and you 'can't do that'. What this tends to do is freak most people out, so much so that they only ever attempt to make the recipe once and then it gets cast aside.

I didn't ever cook by those rules because I wasn't taught by anyone and so was never shown the singular way in which something should be done. I have reworked and retested these recipes to deliver the fastest, simplest and most delicious way to cook them in everyday life without too much stress or a myriad of unnecessary or hard-to-find ingredients.

Over the years, the once-embraced 'simplicity' of food and cookery has been somewhat sidelined in favour of complexity, modernity, technique and process, especially in haute cuisine and fine-dining restaurants. While this is all perfectly valid, I am and shall always remain the consummate home cook, favouring simplicity in ingredients, recipes and techniques, and yet complexity in flavour and depth of satisfaction. So when it comes to recipe creation, I've always prided myself on trying my very best to make my recipes as straightforward as possible, keeping ingredient lists short and unexotic but without compromising the end result, and only garnishing for the purpose of flavour and not visual appeal. If I can strip out an ingredient and still produce a flavourful dish, I will always strive to omit it to keep matters simple, as well as more pocket-friendly.

Over time, I have received a great education from my readers about what they enjoy most about my recipes and it has helped me identify an important framework for them that perhaps wasn't so apparent to me when I first started – everyday dishes that are, for the most part, simple, flavourful and economical, with the occasional special treat thrown in here and there.

As with all my recipes, you can, of course, substitute or omit ingredients to suit your personal tastes – since this is my fifth book, I think you already know this is very much my ethos and that, baking aside, the best recipes usually allow the home cook a little freedom and individuality because, when you keep flavours and proceedings simple, you always produce the best results, and generate confidence and enthusiasm for cooking the type of food you love the most.

So here you have simply good ingredients, simply prepared to create simply wonderful flavours – it really is just that simple.

Simply yours,

Sabrina Ghayour

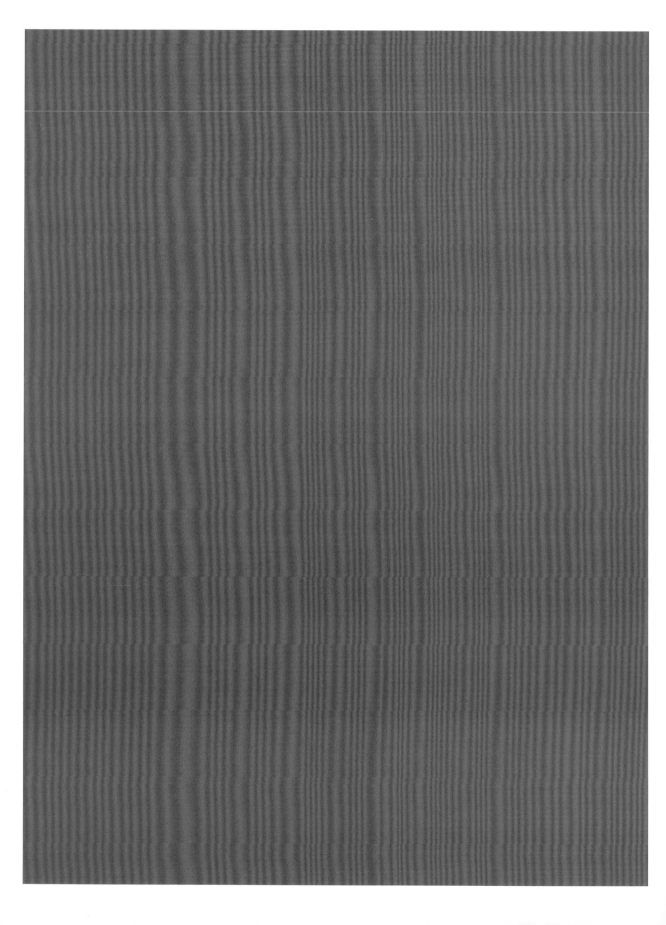

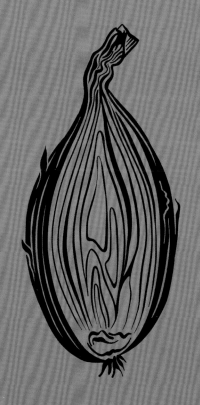

Effortless eating

Thyme & za'atar roasted tomatoes
with strained yogurt balls

Give me a plate of this with a little gently toasted bread, shut the door and leave me in peace. I have always loved tomatoes, but a little herb injection and some honey make this humble dish an absolute game changer. It's the kind of dish that you don't want to plate up individually – you simply want to push your bread about the plate to create different textures and flavours and then mop it all up, and who would blame you? For me, that's the best kind of food.

MAKES 16–18

500g Greek yogurt

500g baby plum tomatoes

1 tablespoon olive oil

2 tablespoons za'atar

4 sprigs of thyme, leaves picked

1 unwaxed lemon, for grating

2 tablespoons runny honey

1 teaspoon pul biber chilli flakes

Maldon sea salt flakes and freshly
ground black pepper

The day before you want to serve, mix the Greek yogurt with 2 tablespoons of salt and then spoon into a muslin bag. Leave to strain over a bowl overnight in the refrigerator.

The next day, preheat the oven to 220°C (200°C fan), Gas Mark 7. Line a baking tray with baking paper.

Place the tomatoes on the prepared baking tray, add the olive oil, za'atar, thyme leaves and salt and pepper and use your hands to mix until the tomatoes are well coated with the oil and seasonings. Roast for 20 minutes until the tomatoes are beginning to char, then remove from the oven and leave to cool.

Remove the strained yogurt from the muslin bag and shape into balls about 3cm in diameter.

Arrange the cooled roasted tomatoes and yogurt balls on a plate. Grate over the zest of the lemon, drizzle over the honey and sprinkle with the pul biber before serving.

SIMPLY DELICIOUS WITH...

Green Bean Salad with Tahini, Preserved Lemon & Pine Nuts (see page 47) and Lamb & Mint Kofte (see page 78).

Mozzarella, olive & za'atar pizzettes

I came up with these when I needed to use up some mozzarella and I resorted to raiding my spice rack. It's a marriage of the Lebanese *mana'eesh* (za'atar-rubbed breads) and the humble Italian pizza, but ultimately very different from both of them. These are stupidly simple and surprisingly delicious – my two favourite qualities in a good recipe.

MAKES 4

4 mini tortilla wraps

olive oil, for drizzling

2 heaped teaspoons za'atar

150g ball of mozzarella (not buffalo
    mozzarella), torn into 1cm pieces

12 Kalamata olives, pitted and sliced

2 tomatoes, cut into 1cm dice

Maldon sea salt flakes and freshly
    ground black pepper

Preheat your oven to its highest setting (with fan if it has one). Line a large baking tray with baking paper.

Place the tortilla wraps on the prepared baking tray and drizzle with just enough olive oil so that when you rub it in it coats the whole wrap. Divide the za'atar between the tortillas, reserving a little for seasoning the topping, then divide the cheese, olives and tomatoes between them.

Season with salt and pepper and the remaining za'atar, then bake for 4–5 minutes until the cheese has melted. Serve immediately.

SIMPLY DELICIOUS WITH...

Green-Yogurt-dressed Baby Gem Lettuce with Burnt Hazelnuts (see page 44) or Marinated Steak with Labneh, Pul Biber Butter & Crispy Onions (see page 188).

Cauliflower & cumin soup

The first time I tried cauliflower soup, no exaggeration, I was head over heels in love with it. I cannot understand why it isn't more popular. Despite cauliflower's delicate nature when cooked, it can handle bold spices extremely well and cumin is really one of the best pairings with it. Soups needn't be a humble affair – they can be rich and decadent as well as comforting, and not just an opening act but very much the star of the show. This example, while simple in terms of ingredients, is a warming wonder of a soup.

SERVES 3—4

1 heaped tablespoon cumin seeds,
   toasted and ground (see Tip)

olive oil

1 large onion, cut into rough chunks

1 large cauliflower, with outer leaves,
   cut into rough chunks

1.5 litres boiling water

150ml double cream

Maldon sea salt flakes and freshly
   ground black pepper

Heat a large saucepan over a medium heat, drizzle in a little olive oil and add the onion and cauliflower along with the ground cumin. Season well with salt and pepper, stir and pour in the boiling water, then cover the pan with a lid and simmer for 20–25 minutes, or until the cauliflower is cooked through. Remove from the heat.

Using a stick blender, blend the mixture to a smooth consistency, adding more water if necessary. Pour in the cream and stir well, then check and adjust the seasoning. Return the soup to the heat and warm through, then serve immediately with bread and garnished with a drizzle of olive oil.

SIMPLY DELICIOUS WITH...

Curry-spiced Parmesan Toasts (see page 19) or Coriander & Feta Spiced Loaf (see page 235).

TIP

To toast spices, heat a dry frying pan over a medium heat and add the spices.
Shake the pan for a minute or so until the spices release their aroma.
Transfer the toasted seeds to a pestle and mortar and grind to a coarse powder.

Spiced carrot & tamarind soup

Carrots make for a wonderful soup but usually with a flavour partner, as on their own their sweetness can be a little overpowering or one-dimensional. Tamarind is a great pairing with the humble carrot, providing it with a rounded acidity that complements but doesn't kill or compete with the vegetable's natural flavour.

SERVES 4—6

olive oil

2 large onions, roughly chopped

1.5kg carrots, peeled and cut
    into rough chunks

1 teaspoon ground cinnamon,
    plus extra to garnish (optional)

1 teaspoon ground turmeric

1 teaspoon ground ginger

1 teaspoon paprika

1 tablespoon garlic granules

1 tablespoon unsweetened tamarind
    paste

1.5 litres boiling water

Maldon sea salt flakes and freshly
    ground black pepper

Place a large saucepan over a medium heat and pour in enough olive oil to coat the base of the pan. Add the onions and carrots and cook for a few minutes, without browning. Add the cinnamon, turmeric, ginger, paprika and garlic granules and stir until the carrots and onions are well coated in the oil and spices. Season with a generous amount of salt and pepper, then add the tamarind paste and the boiling water and stir well.

Reduce the heat to medium-low and gently simmer the soup for 30 minutes, or until the carrots and onions are cooked through. Remove from the heat.

Using a stick blender, blitz the soup until nice and smooth. Check and adjust the seasoning, then serve drizzled with olive oil and sprinkled with a little extra shake of cinnamon, if liked.

SIMPLY DELICIOUS WITH...

Coriander & Feta Spiced Loaf (see page 235).

Curry-spiced Parmesan toasts

I've always been more of a savoury than a sweet girl, especially at breakfast time, but usually at lunch and dinner, too. French toast is something I love, but savoury French toast really is something else, and this little experiment of mine paid off beautifully. Parmesan has such depth of flavour; its intense umami-laden complexity means it can be paired with spice and other feisty ingredients so much more than many other cheeses. It's also the perfect cheese for encrusting these spiced toasts, which I must warn you are rather addictive and not just suited to breakfast; they make a wonderful, lazy supper, too. I love to serve them with a spicy lime pickle chutney or a sweet mango chutney.

MAKES 4

3 eggs

2 teaspoons curry powder

2 teaspoons garlic granules

1 teaspoon cayenne pepper

50ml milk

4 slices of sourdough

50g salted butter

100g Parmesan cheese, finely grated

Maldon sea salt flakes and freshly
    ground black pepper

Put the eggs, curry powder, garlic granules, cayenne, milk and some salt and pepper into a shallow bowl (or food container) and beat together until evenly combined.

Heat a large frying pan over a medium heat. Meanwhile, soak the slices of sourdough in the egg mixture, turning them over to ensure both sides absorb the mixture.

Once the bread has absorbed all the egg mixture, add half the butter to the hot pan, and when melted, fry the first 2 bread slices for 3–4 minutes on the underside. Meanwhile, sprinkle one-quarter of the Parmesan over the top side of each slice and gently press it into the bread, then carefully flip the bread slices over and cook for a further 3–4 minutes until the cheese is melted and golden. Remove from the pan and keep warm under foil (or eat them!) while you repeat with the remaining ingredients, then serve immediately.

SIMPLY DELICIOUS WITH...

Cauliflower & Cumin Soup (see page 15) or Spiced Carrot & Tamarind Soup (see page 16).

Date & ginger chicken wings

Chicken wings will always be one of my all-time favourite things to eat – they're easy on the pocket and great finger food to boot. I am always coming up with new and interesting sauces, marinades and ways to cook them. This is quite a different creation to anything I've ever tasted before, but the one thing I know is that sticky and spicy always make a great flavour combination when it comes to wings, and these don't disappoint. Don't be afraid to let them get nice and deeply charred in the oven – it simply adds to the flavour.

SERVES 4—6

1kg chicken wings

FOR THE MARINADE
250g large dates, pitted and roughly
    chopped
5–7cm piece of fresh root ginger,
    peeled and roughly chopped
2 tablespoons rice vinegar

2 tablespoons garlic oil
1 heaped tablespoon ground ginger
1 tablespoon garlic granules
3 tablespoons boiling water
2 heaped tablespoons Greek yogurt
juice of 1 lemon
Maldon sea salt flakes

Put all the ingredients for the marinade into a food processor with a generous amount of salt and blitz until smooth.

Place the chicken wings in a non-reactive bowl or other container, pour over the marinade, season with salt and pepper, then use your hands to work it into the chicken until well coated. Cover the bowl or container with clingfilm and leave to marinate in the refrigerator for 1 hour, or overnight if liked.

Preheat the oven to 220°C (200°C fan), Gas Mark 7. Line your largest baking tray with baking paper.

Lay the chicken wings on the prepared baking tray and roast for 45 minutes, turning them over halfway through the cooking time, until dark brown, charred on top and cooked through. Serve immediately.

SIMPLY DELICIOUS WITH...
Baked Sweet Potato, Za'atar & Garlic Chips (see page 34) and Tomato & Peanut Salad with Tamarind, Ginger & Honey Dressing (see page 137).

Green chicken

This is what happens when you have a lot of herbs to use up and want to make the quickest roasted chicken for supper. Green chicken has become a bit of a thing in our house, and the herb content has varied wildly, but I have now found a balance I'm happy with. I like to serve these chunks of aromatic, tender chicken in wraps, but they also make a great addition to salads of every description.

SERVES 4—6

650g boneless, skinless chicken breasts, cut into 4cm chunks

FOR THE MARINADE
1 small packet (about 30g) of fresh coriander, roughly chopped
1 small packet (about 30g) of flat leaf parsley, roughly chopped
1 small packet (about 30g) of chives, roughly chopped
2 tablespoons dried dill
1 tablespoon ground fenugreek
1 tablespoon garlic granules

½ teaspoon chilli flakes
4 heaped tablespoons Greek yogurt, plus extra to serve
1 tablespoon olive oil
Maldon sea salt flakes and freshly ground black pepper

TO SERVE
tortilla wraps
tomatoes
sliced red onion
coriander leaves
pul biber chilli flakes

Put all the ingredients for the marinade into a food processor and blitz until you have a smooth purée.

Place the chicken chunks in a mixing bowl, pour the marinade over and mix together well. Cover the bowl with clingfilm and leave the chicken to marinate in the refrigerator overnight. Alternatively, you can bake the chicken as soon as your oven is up to temperature.

Preheat your oven to its highest setting. Line a large baking tray with baking paper.

Spread the chicken out on the prepared baking tray and bake for about 12 minutes until cooked through. Serve immediately in tortilla wraps with more yogurt, tomatoes, sliced red onion, coriander leaves and pul biber.

SIMPLY DELICIOUS WITH...
Baked Sweet Potato, Za'atar & Garlic Chips (see page 34).

Turmeric chicken kebabs

Turmeric really is the key ingredient in this fragrant chicken marinade, which is paired with the vibrant citrus zing of lime and the sweet, rounded finish of honey. These kebabs can be cooked either on the hob, in the oven or on a barbecue (see Tip), and they are so versatile they can be served with wraps, rice, fries or even just on their own.

SERVES 4—6

4 boneless, skinless chicken breasts
(about 650g total weight)
sweet chilli sauce, to serve

FOR THE MARINADE
5cm piece of fresh turmeric,
scrubbed and finely grated
1 tablespoon garlic granules

finely grated zest and juice of
1 unwaxed lime
2 tablespoons natural yogurt
1 generous tablespoon clear honey
1 tablespoon olive oil
Maldon sea salt flakes and freshly
ground black pepper

Put all the ingredients for the marinade into a plastic food container and mix together.

Cut each chicken breast lengthways into 3 equal long strips. Add to the marinade in the food container and seal with the lid. Shake well to coat the chicken in the marinade. Leave to marinate in the refrigerator for 30 minutes–1 hour, or overnight if liked.

Thread each strip of marinated chicken on to small wooden or metal skewers. Cook in a griddle pan over a high heat for 3–4 minutes on each side or until nicely browned and cooked through.

Alternatively, preheat your oven to its highest setting (with fan if it has one). Line a large baking tray with baking paper. Lay the kebabs on the prepared baking tray and bake for 10–12 minutes or until cooked through. Serve immediately with sweet chilli sauce.

SIMPLY DELICIOUS WITH...
Sweetcorn, Black Bean & Avocado Salad (see page 139) or Polow-e-Bademjan-o-Felfel (see page 125).

TIP
You can also cook these kebabs over a barbecue. If using wooden skewers, soak them in water for 30 minutes before using. Cook over a medium-low heat for about 5–6 minutes on each side until nicely browned and cooked through.

Pomegranate shallots

Roasted shallots have always been one of my favourite accompaniments to roasted meats. There is something about their sweet, soft flesh that I love mashing up and mixing with every bite of my meal – I could eat a whole tray of them, to be honest. This version is slightly different, as the pomegranate molasses adds quite a tart flavour to contrast with the natural sweetness of the shallots. I would suggest making a double quantity if there are more than two of you, as it's really worth it and involves little extra effort. The final flourish of sumac gives the dish a pronounced citric bite, just as the pomegranate molasses has intensified and sweetened it.

SERVES 2–4

3 tablespoons pomegranate molasses

1 generous tablespoon clear honey

1 teaspoon ground cinnamon

400g long shallots, peeled but kept whole

1 teaspoon sumac

Maldon sea salt flakes and freshly ground black pepper

Preheat the oven to 200°C (180°C fan), Gas Mark 6.

Select an ovenproof dish that accommodates all the shallots tightly with no room to spare.

In a small bowl, mix together the pomegranate molasses, honey, cinnamon and a generous amount of salt and pepper until evenly combined.

Lay the shallots in the ovenproof dish and pour over the sauce. Don't worry if the sauce doesn't cling to the shallots at this uncooked stage.

Roast the shallots for 1 hour 20 minutes, basting them every 20 minutes. Sprinkle the sumac on top for the final 20 minutes of cooking. When cooked the shallots should be tender and easily pierced with a sharp knife. Remove from the oven and serve immediately.

SIMPLY DELICIOUS WITH...

Spice-rubbed Spatchcocked Poussin (see page 55) or Pot-roasted Brisket with Harissa & Spices (see page 59).

Charred courgettes
with lemon, oregano & pul biber

This is one of my regular, quick summer vegetable dishes – an absolute lazy staple in my house. I wholeheartedly encourage you to nicely char the courgettes because it makes them so moreish and delicious. I love using this oven method – high temperature, short cooking time – which gives such a pleasing result for so many different ingredients, from courgettes and peppers to chicken and salmon. The lemon juice brings a wonderful finish to the spicy, charred courgettes, and you can enjoy them hot or cold and even add a little feta to serve.

SERVES 4–6

4 courgettes
olive or garlic oil, for drizzling
finely grated zest of 1 unwaxed lemon
    and juice of ½
2 tablespoons dried wild oregano
1 teaspoon pul biber chilli flakes
Maldon sea salt flakes and freshly
    ground black pepper

Preheat your oven to its highest setting. Line your largest baking tray with baking paper.

Cut the courgettes diagonally into 1cm-thick slices and spread them out on the prepared baking tray. Drizzle with a generous amount of olive or garlic oil and sprinkle over all the remaining ingredients, except the lemon juice. Season generously with salt and pepper and then rub the seasonings all over the courgette slices.

Roast the courgettes for 8 minutes, then remove from the oven, squeeze the lemon juice evenly over the courgettes and roast for a further 6 minutes before serving.

SIMPLY DELICIOUS WITH...

Turmeric Chicken Kebabs (see page 24) or Sea Bream with Spiced Green Olive & Shallot Butter (see page 64).

Cannellini bean mash
with preserved lemon & tahini

I have a lot of love for the humble bean in every guise – salads, stews, soups, dips and patties. While versatile and flavoursome, they often need an additional gentle flavour pairing to bring out the best in them. Here, I've turned to much bolder flavours, which nevertheless work quite subtly with the cannellini beans, but every now and again you get the most wonderful sharp spike of preserved lemon that complements their creamy, sweet nature so well.

SERVES 4—6

500g dried cannellini beans

3 tablespoons olive oil, plus extra
   for drizzling

2 heaped tablespoons tahini

3 garlic cloves, minced

4–5 tablespoons warm water, or
   more if needed

6 preserved lemons, deseeded and
   finely chopped

1 small packet (about 30g) of flat leaf
   parsley, leaves and stalks finely
   chopped

Maldon sea salt flakes, if needed,
   and freshly ground black pepper

Soak the cannellini beans in cold water for 8–10 hours or overnight, then drain.

Cook the beans in a saucepan of boiling water for 1½ hours or until cooked, topping up the water as necessary.

Drain the cooked beans and return them to the pan. Add the olive oil, tahini and garlic and mash the beans roughly over a gentle heat until mashed to your preferred texture.

Pour in the warm water (add more if you prefer a looser consistency), season well with pepper and mix in the preserved lemons and parsley. Check the seasoning and add a tiny bit of salt if needed, bearing in mind that preserved lemons are in themselves a little salty. Serve immediately drizzled with extra olive oil.

SIMPLY DELICIOUS WITH...

Pot-roasted Brisket with Harissa & Spices (see page 59) or Sea Bream with Spiced Green Olive & Shallot Butter (see page 64).

Slow-cooked butter beans
with oregano, tomatoes & garlic

I am a recent convert to dried beans and sometimes they really are worth the extra time. I like a little bite in my beans, which canned beans lack, so this garlicky, sauce-laden baked delight is one example where your time is well spent. It's hearty but not heavy, rich – but only in a really good way – and ideal for sharing.

SERVES 4—6

250g dried butter beans

250g baby plum tomatoes, halved

4–6 garlic cloves, peeled and bashed but kept whole

generous handful of fresh oregano, roughly chopped

1 heaped tablespoon tomato purée

2 teaspoons dried oregano

1 teaspoon chilli flakes

50g butter

4 tablespoons olive oil

about 700ml cold water

generous amount of Maldon sea salt flakes and freshly ground black pepper

crusty bread, to serve (optional)

Soak the butter beans in cold water for 8–10 hours or overnight, then drain.

Preheat the oven to 180°C (160°C fan), Gas Mark 4.

Select a rectangular ovenproof dish, about 32 x 24cm. Add all the ingredients, except the water, to the dish and mix together well, then pour over the cold water, or enough to ensure the beans are immersed.

Bake for 2 hours until the beans are completely soft, checking after 1½ hours and topping up the water if necessary. Serve hot, with crusty bread if liked.

SIMPLY DELICIOUS WITH...

Maast-o-Esfenaj (see page 72) or Beetroot & Feta Lattice (see page 67).

TIP

If you have any leftovers, lightly mash them the next day for something completely different.

Baked sweet potato, za'atar & garlic chips

I can quite happily sit in front of a mountain of any kind of cooked sweet potato and work my way through the entire lot with the greatest of ease. I find its light, digestible nature almost dangerously appealing. These are just that, dangerously appealing, although there is actually little danger here because, as we know, sweet potatoes are good for us and baking them makes them even less sinful. The only danger is that, much like me, you'll nail half the tray before they have even hit the plate… but then again, that's not such a bad thing.

SERVES 4—6

3 tablespoons quick-cook polenta

3 tablespoons za'atar

1 heaped tablespoon garlic granules

4 sweet potatoes, peeled and cut into
    1cm-thick chips

3 tablespoons olive oil

Maldon sea salt flakes and freshly
    ground black pepper

Preheat the oven to 220°C (200°C fan), Gas Mark 7. Line your largest baking tray with baking paper.

Mix the polenta, za'atar, garlic granules and a generous amount of salt and pepper together in a small bowl.

Place the sweet potato chips on the prepared baking tray, drizzle over the olive oil and use your hands to mix until the chips are well coated in the oil. Sprinkle with the polenta and seasoning mixture and toss to coat the chips evenly.

Spread the chips out on the baking tray and bake for about 30 minutes until soft in the middle and the edges start to brown. Serve immediately.

SIMPLY DELICIOUS WITH…

Turmeric Chicken Kebabs (see page 24) or Crispy Cod Wraps with Salsa & Harissa Lime Mayo (see page 160).

Spiced turmeric mashed potatoes
with coriander

I've always loved mashed potato, but this is the next level taste-wise. It's so comforting, and I'm not sure how it could be improved. I am mad about turmeric and it's no secret that I love chilli, and the natural sweetness of the potatoes means they can handle the spices and chilli heat easily. This is a dish I can't recommend enough, even if you are simply looking for an alternative to your usual mashed potato side.

SERVES 6—8

2kg floury potatoes, peeled and halved, or quartered if large

1 teaspoon cumin seeds

1 teaspoon black mustard seeds

100g butter

1—2 teaspoons chilli flakes, to taste

20g fresh turmeric, scrubbed and very finely grated

1 small packet (about 30g) of fresh coriander, finely chopped

Maldon sea salt flakes and freshly ground black pepper

Cook the potatoes in a large saucepan of salted boiling water for 15–20 minutes, or until cooked through. Drain in a colander and set aside to steam dry.

Place the saucepan over a medium heat, add the cumin and mustard seeds and toast them, shaking the pan, for a few minutes until they release their aroma. Add the butter, chilli flakes and turmeric and stir until the butter has melted.

Return the potatoes to the pan and season with a generous amount of salt and pepper, then mash with the spiced butter until just combined – I like my mash to have some chunky texture. Check and adjust the seasoning, and when you're happy with it, add the coriander and mix well, then serve.

SIMPLY DELICIOUS WITH...

Spice-rubbed Spatchcocked Poussin (see page 55) or Yogurt & Spice Roasted Salmon (see page 62).

TIP
Any leftovers make a fantastic filling for a toastie with lots of grated mature Cheddar cheese – carb heaven!

Tomato & garlic rice

This is my kind of quick and lazy rice – especially when I'm cooking many other dishes at the same time or simply too tired to cook rice the Persian way – and a handy one that uses store-cupboard ingredients to bring it together. It's a full-flavoured recipe that I find myself turning to time and again, and makes a great accompaniment to roasts and stews.

SERVES 4

250g basmati rice

1 red onion, halved and very thinly sliced
    into half moons

4 garlic cloves, minced

1 small packet (about 30g) of flat leaf parsley,
    finely chopped

50g butter

4 heaped tablespoons tomato purée

1 heaped teaspoon garlic granules

1 teaspoon ground coriander

finely grated zest and juice of 1 fat unwaxed lime

400ml cold water

Maldon sea salt flakes and freshly ground
    black pepper

Put all the ingredients into a saucepan with a lid, season with a generous amount of salt and pepper and stir together well.

If using a gas hob, place over a low heat, or if using an electric/induction hob place over a medium-low heat. Cover the pan with the lid and cook for about 30 minutes, or until the rice on the top is tender and cooked through and all the water has been fully absorbed.

SIMPLY DELICIOUS WITH...

Spiced Pork Stew (see page 185) or Turmeric & Black Pepper Braised Lamb Neck (see page 96).

Spring onion salad
with sesame & pul biber

Persians love onions of every description; we eat spring onions and onions raw as accompaniments to our meals. This salad is one that I can quite happily eat on the side of roasted meats, stews, sandwiches and much more – it just seems to go with so many things, and it's ridiculously easy to make, too.

SERVES 4—6

2 teaspoons sesame seeds

2 tablespoons caster sugar

2 teaspoons rice vinegar

2 teaspoons sesame oil

2 teaspoons pul biber chilli flakes

2 bunches of spring onions, thinly sliced
    diagonally from root to tip

Maldon sea salt flakes and freshly ground
    black pepper

Put the sesame seeds, sugar, rice vinegar and sesame oil into a large mixing bowl and stir well until the sugar dissolves. Stir in the pul biber.

Add the spring onions and toss to coat in the dressing.

Season well with salt and pepper, toss again and serve.

SIMPLY DELICIOUS WITH...

Yogurt & Spice Roasted Salmon (see page 62).

Flame-roasted pepper, pistachio & dill yogurt

We Eastern types are slightly obsessed with yogurt. It's a staple of the table, whether served plain or combined with cucumber, spinach or beetroot, and an essential for any serious meal in an Eastern household. While roasted peppers don't feature heavily in Persian cuisine, I very much love the texture and they always remind me of sun-soaked destinations like Turkey or Greece. The added crunch from the pistachios makes this less of a dip and more of a dish in itself. Lightly toast or chargrill some of your favourite bread and use it as a vessel to scoop this up.

SERVES 4—6

450g jar (170g drained weight) red or mixed-coloured flame-roasted peppers, drained and patted dry
1 long shallot, very finely chopped
1 garlic clove, minced
500g Greek yogurt
1 small packet (about 30g) of dill, very finely chopped

50g pistachio slivers (or very roughly chopped whole nuts)
olive oil, for drizzling
Maldon sea salt flakes and freshly ground black pepper

Thinly slice the peppers widthways into ribbons. Put them into a mixing bowl along with the shallot and garlic and give them a mix.

Add the yogurt, dill, pistachios, some salt and a generous amount of pepper, then drizzle with about 1 tablespoon olive oil and mix together well. Leave to sit for about 5 minutes and then check and adjust the seasoning to taste.

Spread the yogurt mixture on to a large plate, add a little extra drizzle of olive oil and a grinding of pepper and serve.

SIMPLY DELICIOUS WITH...

Pomegranate Molasses & Honey-glazed Meatballs (see page 56) or Albaloo Polow (see page 89).

Green-yogurt-dressed Baby Gem lettuce *with burnt hazelnuts*

If I'm going to eat salad, it has to have lots of flavour, texture and substance to it in order to win me over. This one is deceptively simple, and I can quite easily demolish half of it in a matter of minutes. The darkly toasted hazelnuts really add something wonderful to it, but the fresh herb-packed dressing is what makes it so good. To make this dish more of a meal, you can crumble a little feta on top or add cooked chicken if liked.

SERVES 6–8

50g blanched hazelnuts

4 heads of Baby Gem lettuce, quartered

2–3 small preserved lemons, deseeded and finely chopped

Maldon sea salt flakes and freshly ground black pepper

FOR THE DRESSING

½ small packet (about 15g) of dill

½ small packet (about 15g) of flat leaf parsley

½ small packet (about 15g) of basil

3 heaped tablespoons Greek yogurt

1 tablespoon olive oil

1–2 tablespoons cold water (depending how thick your yogurt is), optional

Preheat the oven to 220°C (200°C fan), Gas Mark 7.

Spread the hazelnuts out on a baking tray and toast in the oven for 6–7 minutes until darkly toasted. Remove from the oven and leave to cool.

Put all the ingredients for the dressing, except the water, into a blender. Season with salt and pepper and blitz until smooth and vibrant green. Add the cold water if needed to thin down to a pouring consistency.

Arrange the lettuce quarters on a platter and pour the dressing over, then scatter all over with the chopped preserved lemons. Season well with pepper, top with the toasted hazelnuts and serve immediately.

SIMPLY DELICIOUS WITH...

Beetroot & Feta Lattice (see page 67) or Green & Black-eyed Bean Baklava with Feta & Honey (see page 193).

Green bean salad
with tahini, preserved lemon & pine nuts

Green beans are so versatile; I use them in stir-fries, stews, rice, soups and especially in salads, as they are a great carrier of flavours and dressings. Tahini is a marvellous ingredient, but it does need other additions to make it shine, and usually a hit of lemon does the trick beautifully. This wonderful green bean salad is spiked with tangy, salty preserved lemon slices and crunchy pine nuts to create an ideal side dish as well as a perfect lunchbox option to take to work the next day.

SERVES 4

400g fine green beans
2 preserved lemons
1 fat garlic clove, minced
generous squeeze of lemon juice
1 tablespoon tahini
3 tablespoons warm water
handful of pine nuts
freshly ground black pepper

Cook the green beans in a saucepan of boiling water for about 10–12 minutes, or according to the packet instructions – the timing will vary depending on their variety and thickness. Drain and rinse under cold running water until cool, then drain well and dry on kitchen paper.

Cut the preserved lemons in half and thinly slice them into half moons. Set aside.

Put the garlic into a small bowl with the lemon juice. Add the tahini and then mix in the warm water to loosen the mixture – don't use cold water, or the mixture will seize.

Place the green beans in a mixing bowl and pour the dressing over. Add the preserved lemon slices and season with a generous amount of pepper, then transfer to a plate and scatter with the pine nuts before serving.

SIMPLY DELICIOUS WITH...

Ultimate Falafels (see page 81) or Harissa Chicken Noodle Lettuce Cups (see page 115).

Cucumber, green apple & nigella salad *with feta & dill*

Feta is always a wonderful addition to a salad but here it acts more as a dressing than an ingredient. The refreshing combination of cooling cucumber and sharp yet sweet apple makes it the perfect side dish for so many different meals. Alternatively, you can chop the apple and cucumber finely and serve a dollop on chicory leaves as a light snack.

SERVES 6—8

100g feta cheese

3 tablespoons Greek yogurt

2 teaspoons nigella seeds

2 Granny Smith apples, cored, halved and sliced into half moons

1 large cucumber, peeled, halved lengthways and seeds scooped out, then cut into 5mm-thick slices

1 small packet (about 30g) of dill, finely chopped

Maldon sea salt flakes and freshly ground black pepper

1 spring onion, sliced diagonally, to garnish

olive oil, for drizzling

Mash the feta into a paste in a mixing bowl. Add the Greek yogurt, a little salt and a generous amount of pepper and mix together well.

Add 1½ teaspoons of the nigella seeds, the apples, cucumber and dill, then toss the ingredients in the feta mixture until evenly coated.

Arrange the salad on a serving platter, sprinkle over the remaining nigella seeds and garnish with the spring onion, then drizzle with a little olive oil before serving.

SIMPLY DELICIOUS WITH...

Fragrant Fish Cakes with Preserved Lemon Mayonnaise (see page 152) or Seafood, Coconut & Ginger Spiced Rice (see page 156).

Carrot, pistachio & dill salad
with lime & honey dressing

Although I love carrots, I have to confess that I often just peel them and eat them raw on their own or use as a vehicle for hummus. This is a lovely, yet simple, salad with lots of flavour and a nutty flourish of pistachio, too. Texture is a big thing for me and one of the humble carrot's greatest gifts – in addition to its sweet flavour – is that wonderful, juicy crunch.

SERVES 4—6

500g carrots, peeled and shredded in a food processor or coarsely grated

½ small red onion, halved and thinly sliced into half moons

75g pistachio nuts, roughly chopped

1 small packet (about 30g) of dill, finely chopped

2 teaspoons nigella seeds

FOR THE DRESSING

2 tablespoons olive oil

finely grated zest and juice of 1 unwaxed lime

1 generous tablespoon clear honey

generous amount of Maldon sea salt flakes and freshly ground black pepper

Mix all the dressing ingredients together in a small jug.

Place all the salad ingredients in a large mixing bowl. When ready to serve, add the dressing to the salad and use your hands to very gently toss in the dressing until evenly coated. Check and adjust the seasoning to taste. Serve immediately.

SIMPLY DELICIOUS WITH...

Steak Tartines with Tarragon & Paprika Butter (see page 129) or Chicken & Apricot Pastries (see page 169).

TIP
Make sure to add the dressing just before serving to avoid the carrots from going soggy. If you're vegan, you can substitute the honey with agave syrup.

Fennel salad
with spinach, cashew & coriander seed dressing

My love for fennel was a slow-burner, but over time I have learned to wholeheartedly embrace all the ways in which it can be enjoyed. I've already written several fennel recipes and I very much wanted to come up with one that was totally different to the more common ways of preparing it, so this particular combination is like nothing you've ever tried before. The cashew nuts give the dressing a lovely texture so that the fennel is entirely enrobed in a rich, satisfying sauce.

SERVES 4—6

2 large fennel bulbs

FOR THE DRESSING
125g baby spinach leaves
125g cashew nuts
3 teaspoons sumac, plus 1 teaspoon
   to garnish
2 teaspoons ground coriander

2 teaspoons coriander seeds, toasted
   (see Tip on page 15)
4 tablespoons olive oil
2 tablespoons lukewarm water
2 tablespoons red wine vinegar
Maldon sea salt flakes and freshly
   ground black pepper

Put all the dressing ingredients, except the 1 teaspoon sumac to garnish, into a food processor and blitz until you have a sauce consistency. Add an extra tablespoon of water to thin down if necessary.

Trim the fennel bulbs, then quarter and thinly slice them. Put the fennel into a mixing bowl, pour the dressing over and toss until each slice of fennel is well coated.

Arrange the fennel salad on a plate, sprinkle with the remaining sumac and serve.

SIMPLY DELICIOUS WITH...
Chorizo, Goats' Cheese & Cumin Borek (see page 148) or Tahchin (see page 87).

Spice-rubbed spatchcocked poussin

The joy of a poussin is that it cooks in half the time of a normal-sized chicken. Spatchcocking a poussin reduces the cooking time further still and makes for a wonderful, evenly cooked bird with lovely crisp skin and juicy, tender meat. If that's not fast food, then I don't know what is.

SERVES 2—4

2 poussins

FOR THE MARINADE
2 garlic cloves, minced
2 tablespoons dried marjoram
1 tablespoon coriander seeds, toasted
    and ground (see Tip on page 15)
1 teaspoon chilli flakes

1 teaspoon ground black pepper
3 tablespoons olive oil
juice of ½ lemon
Maldon sea salt flakes

TO SERVE
bread
rocket salad

Line a baking tray with baking paper.

To spatchcock the poussins, place each bird in turn breast side down on a chopping board. Using a good pair of kitchen scissors, cut down either side of the backbone and then remove the bone. Lay breast side up on the prepared baking tray and gently press down on each bird with both hands until as flat as possible.

Mix all the marinade ingredients together in a small bowl or jug, then pour over the poussins and rub in all over. Cover the tray with clingflim and leave to marinate in the refrigerator for 1 hour, or overnight, if liked.

Preheat the oven to 220°C (200°C fan), Gas Mark 7.

Roast the birds for about 30 minutes or until cooked through and nicely browned with crispy skin – the juices should run clear when the thickest part of the meat is pierced with the tip of a sharp knife. Remove from the oven and leave to rest for 10 minutes before serving with bread and a rocket salad.

SIMPLY DELICIOUS WITH...

Cannellini Bean Mash with Preserved Lemon & Tahini (see page 31) or Roasted Parsnips with Tahini Yogurt Sauce, Herb Oil & Pomegranate Seeds (see page 177).

Pomegranate molasses & honey-glazed meatballs

Essentially, these meatballs are a total spice-cupboard raid, but what really brings them to life and sets them apart from my other recipes is the addition of pomegranate molasses. It's an ingredient that works so well with red meat and game, as it cuts through any richness effortlessly and makes for such a wonderful and somewhat exotic flavour combination. I have always drizzled pomegranate molasses on to tomatoes, salads, kebabs and grills, so it was only a matter of time before I paired it with meatballs, too.

MAKES ABOUT 24—28 MEATBALLS

500g minced beef (20% fat)

1 onion, minced in a food processor and drained of any liquid, or very finely chopped

1 small packet (about 30g) of flat leaf parsley, finely chopped

1 tablespoon garlic granules

1 teaspoon ground cumin

1 teaspoon ground coriander

1 teaspoon ground cinnamon

1 teaspoon Maldon sea salt flakes, crumbled

vegetable oil, for frying

FOR THE GLAZE

4 tablespoons pomegranate molasses

2 tablespoons clear honey

Put all the main ingredients, except the vegetable oil, into a large mixing bowl and, using your hands, work them together really well, pummelling the meat mixture for several minutes into a smooth paste.

Line a plate with kitchen paper. Shape the mixture into 24–28 evenly-sized meatballs.

Heat a large frying pan over a medium-high heat. Once the pan is hot, add a drizzle of vegetable oil and fry the meatballs in batches for 8–10 minutes until browned all over and cooked through. Remove from the pan with a slotted spoon and transfer to the paper-lined plate to drain.

Wipe out the pan with kitchen paper and return to the hob over a medium heat. Add the pomegranate molasses and honey to the pan and stir. Return the meatballs to the pan and turn them in the glaze until well coated. Cook until the glaze has reduced to a sticky coating , then serve immediately.

SIMPLY DELICIOUS WITH...

Tomato & Garlic Rice (see page 38) or Polow-e-Bademjan-o-Felfel (see page 125).

Pot-roasted brisket
with harissa & spices

One-pot cooking is a joy, and this little beauty never disappoints. From a cook's perspective, nothing could be easier than this recipe, and from the diner's perspective, it's ridiculously juicy, tender and packs in plenty of flavour. Should you, for some unknown reason, have any left over, it makes a wonderful stew or sandwich or pie filling, or combine any leftovers with a can of coconut milk and serve over rice for the most rewarding bowl of comfort food.

SERVES 6—8

750ml cold water

2 heaped tablespoons rose harissa

1 teaspoon ground turmeric

1 teaspoon ground cumin

1 teaspoon ground cinnamon

1 teaspoon ground fenugreek

2.5kg rolled beef brisket joint

Maldon sea salt flakes and freshly
  ground black pepper

Preheat the oven to 160°C (140°C fan), Gas Mark 3.

Measure the cold water in a measuring jug, add the harissa and ground spices with a generous amount of salt and pepper and stir until the ingredients are evenly combined.

Place the beef in an ovenproof casserole dish with a lid and pour in the spiced liquid. Cook, uncovered, for 2 hours, basting regularly.

Cover the dish with the lid and cook for a further 2 hours, again basting the meat from time to time, then remove the lid and cook the beef for a further 1 hour before serving.

SIMPLY DELICIOUS WITH...

Pomegranate Shallots (see page 27) and Spiced Turmeric Mashed Potatoes with Coriander (see page 37).

TIP

This is also fabulous with mashed root vegetables or shredded and served with flatbreads, yogurt and a dash of pomegranate molasses, pomegranate seeds and some fresh herbs such as mint.

Smoky beef, potato & pea pan-fry
with eggs & yogurt

Every once in a while, laziness prevails and I want something that can be made and served in the same pan and then placed in the centre of the table to be shared. I like to take the time to fry the potatoes properly, as they really are the star of the show.

SERVES 4

600g potatoes, peeled and cut into
    2cm cubes
vegetable oil, for frying
1 heaped teaspoon cumin seeds
1 onion, finely chopped
500g minced beef
1 teaspoon garlic granules
1 teaspoon smoked paprika
1 teaspoon ground turmeric
1 teaspoon sumac

2 handfuls of frozen peas
1 small packet (about 30g) of flat leaf
    parsley, roughly chopped
4 eggs
Maldon sea salt flakes and freshly
    ground black pepper

TO SERVE
Greek or natural yogurt
your favourite chilli sauce (optional)

Rinse the potato cubes in cold water, drain well and pat dry with kitchen paper.

Line a plate with a double layer of kitchen paper. Heat a frying pan over a medium-high heat and pour in enough oil to coat the base of the pan. Add the potatoes, spreading them out into a single layer, and fry for about 12–15 minutes until cooked through, turning the pieces over as they cook to ensure they all brown evenly and adding the cumin seeds once a couple of sides have browned. Remove with a slotted spoon and transfer to the paper-lined plate to drain.

Add the onion to the pan and fry for a few minutes until nicely browned, then add the minced beef and mix with the onion. Stir in the garlic granules, spices and some salt and pepper and cook for a few minutes until the beef is cooked through. Add the frozen peas and cook, stirring, for a few minutes, then stir through the parsley and the fried potatoes. Next, make 4 wells in the mixture and crack an egg into each. Cover the pan with a lid and cook for 5–7 minutes, or until the eggs are cooked to your liking. Season with black pepper, then serve straight from the pan with Greek or natural yogurt and your favourite chilli sauce, if liked.

Yogurt & spice roasted salmon

I love to cook salmon in the oven. It's lazy, quick, works really well and you don't need any oil, as salmon is naturally fatty and delicious. These little salmon bites are something I've made time and time again over the years and this method of roasting them at a high temperature ensures you get a little charring on the outside yet perfectly cooked salmon on the inside. Leftovers also make a great addition to your lunchbox the next day.

SERVES 4

500g skinless salmon fillet, cut into
    4cm cubes

FOR THE MARINADE
4 tablespoons Greek yogurt
1 tablespoon garlic granules
1 heaped tablespoon rose harissa
1 teaspoon ground turmeric
1 teaspoon paprika
finely grated zest of 1 unwaxed lime
    and a good squeeze of juice

1 teaspoon olive oil
generous amount of Maldon sea salt
    flakes and freshly ground black
    pepper

TO SERVE
tortilla wraps
sliced tomatoes
finely sliced onion
coriander leaves
Greek yogurt

Preheat your oven to its highest setting (with fan if it has one). Line a baking tray with baking paper.

Mix all the marinade ingredients together in a mixing bowl. Add the salmon and turn until well coated in the marinade.

Spread the salmon out on the prepared baking tray and roast for 10 minutes until cooked through. Remove from the oven and serve immediately with tortilla wraps, tomatoes, finely sliced onion, coriander leaves and Greek yogurt.

SIMPLY DELICIOUS WITH...
Maast-o-Esfenaj (see page 72) or Baked Sweet Potato, Za'atar & Garlic Chips (see page 34).

Sea bream
with spiced green olive & shallot butter

As a child I wasn't the biggest lover of fish. It might be a Persian thing, as fish doesn't tend to feature heavily in the traditional Persian diet, unless you live by the sea, which may explain why we can be tricky to please. These days I am mad about fish of every description; the older I get, the more I enjoy it and tend to choose it when eating out. It is light, digestible and an excellent carrier of flavour, so long as you don't overpower a delicate variety. Sea bream is one that can handle a little flavour bomb, and this simple but effective spiced butter is just that – an explosion of flavour that just works incredibly well with the fish.

SERVES 2—4

4 tablespoons olive oil

4 skin-on sea bream fillets,
    about 100g each

50g butter

16 green olives, pitted and
    finely chopped

1 small shallot, very finely chopped

1 heaped teaspoon sumac

1 heaped teaspoon pul biber chilli flakes

Maldon sea salt flakes and freshly
    ground black pepper

Heat a frying pan over a medium-high heat. Once hot, drizzle in 1 tablespoon of the olive oil, add 2 sea bream fillets, skin side down, and fry for 2–3 minutes until the skin crisps up, then carefully turn them over and cook for a further minute. Remove from the pan and keep warm under foil. Repeat with the remaining sea bream fillets.

Wipe the pan out with kitchen paper and return to a gentle heat. Add the remaining 2 tablespoons olive oil and the butter, and once melted, add the olives and shallot and stir for 1–2 minutes to heat through. Season generously with salt and pepper, then add the sumac and pul biber and stir. Pour the spiced butter over the fish and serve immediately.

SIMPLY DELICIOUS WITH...

Cannellini Bean Mash with Preserved Lemon & Tahini (see page 31) and Charred Courgettes with Lemon, Oregano & Pul Biber (see page 28).

Beetroot & feta lattice

It's no secret that I always keep vacuum-packed cooked beetroot and feta cheese in my refrigerator at all times. They have saved me from going hungry on many occasions and are actually rather wonderful paired together, especially in salads. But sometimes, and especially in winter, you want something warm and comforting, so you might say this recipe is inevitable when you also find yourself with a spare packet of puff pastry. That perfect balance of a sweet, salty and creamy filling encased in puff pastry is comfort food personified. Hot or cold, side dish or main, it's a winner.

SERVES 4–6

400g vacuum-packed cooked beetroot in natural juice (or peeled, cooked whole fresh beetroots)

1 heaped teaspoon dried wild oregano

1 teaspoon chilli flakes

300g vegetarian feta cheese

1 x 320g ready-rolled all-butter puff pastry sheet

beaten egg, to glaze

freshly ground black pepper

Preheat the oven to 200°C (180°C fan), Gas Mark 6. Line a baking tray with baking paper.

Coarsely grate the beetroot. Place in a sieve and squeeze out as much of the beetroot's juices as you can without mashing it. Tip into a mixing bowl with the oregano, chilli flakes and a generous amount of pepper, then loosely crumble in the feta and give everything a good mix.

Cut the pastry sheet in half lengthways to form 2 long rectangles (one for base of the lattice and one for the top). Lay the pastry base on the prepared baking tray and spoon the filling along its length, then use your hands to neatly pack and compress the filling into a sausage shape, leaving a 1cm border of pastry.

Take the pastry top and make a series of small diagonal cuts in rows, leaving a 3cm border of uncut pastry (or cut an alternative pattern of your choosing). Lay the pastry top over the filling, carefully stretching it to cover the filling, then tuck the edges underneath the pastry base to neaten and hide the seam. Press the edges down firmly to seal, then brush beaten egg over all the exposed pastry. Bake for 25–30 minutes, or until the pastry is deep golden brown. Remove from the oven and serve hot or cold, cut into slices.

SIMPLY DELICIOUS WITH...

Pear, Chickpea & Green Leaf Salad with Maple Harissa Dressing (see page 172).

Roasted nectarines
with labneh, herbs & honey

Is it a salad? Is it a dessert? The truth is, I just don't know. One thing I do know for sure is that it's absolutely delicious. It's a dish that people circle around apprehensively not knowing how to tackle, but once they do, it's gone pretty quickly. Fruity, savoury, crunchy, spicy and sweet – the kind of combination that simply cannot fail to please.

SERVES 4—6

4 large ripe nectarines, halved
    and stoned
olive oil, for drizzling
500g labneh, or Greek yogurt
    strained in a muslin bag overnight
    (see page 11)
generous handful of toasted flaked
    almonds

1 heaped teaspoon dried wild oregano
1 heaped teaspoon pul biber chilli flakes
2 tablespoons clear honey
handful of mint leaves, stacked, rolled up
    together and finely sliced widthways
    into thin ribbons
Maldon sea salt flakes and freshly ground
    black pepper

Preheat the oven to 220°C (200°C fan), Gas Mark 7. Line a large baking tray with baking paper.

Place the nectarine halves cut side up on the prepared tray, then drizzle each with a little olive oil and season generously with pepper. Bake for 25–30 minutes until the edges of the fruit are browned and the flesh is cooked through and tender. Remove from the oven and leave to cool.

Select a large platter and spread the labneh or strained Greek yogurt all over the surface, then arrange the roasted nectarines on top. Drizzle with a little olive oil, season with a little salt and sprinkle over the toasted flaked almonds, followed by the oregano and pul biber. Drizzle all over with the honey and, finally, scatter over the mint ribbons. Take to the table to serve.

SIMPLY DELICIOUS WITH...

Lamb & Mint Kofte (see page 78) or Spiced Chicory & Roasted Pepper Salad with Oranges & Anchovies (see page 180).

Traditions with a twist

Maast-o-esfenaj
spinach & yogurt with walnuts

This is a much-loved staple of Persian cuisine. Traditionally, we don't add garlic or sumac, and walnuts may be used to garnish the top, but I like to add them to the dish for texture. This is the one dish that always surprises my students at my Persian cookery class, as yogurt is always thought of as a dip in the West, while the Persians treat it as a main event but also as a condiment that goes with or over everything, or it can be simply enjoyed on its own.

SERVES 6–8

250g spinach leaves

500g thick Greek yogurt

1 large garlic clove, minced

2 generous handfuls of walnut halves, roughly chopped

2 teaspoons sumac, plus extra to garnish

olive oil, for drizzling

Maldon sea salt flakes and freshly ground black pepper

flatbread, to serve

Bring a saucepan of water to the boil, add the spinach and simmer for 2–3 minutes until wilted, then drain and plunge into a bowl of iced water to stop it from cooking further. Once cooled, drain well and finely chop.

Put the spinach into a mixing bowl with the yogurt, garlic, walnuts (reserving some for garnish), sumac, a little drizzle of olive oil and a generous amount of salt and pepper. Mix together well.

Spread the mixture out on a flat plate, then drizzle with olive oil and sprinkle with extra sumac and the reserved walnuts before serving.

SIMPLY DELICIOUS WITH...

Yogurt & Spice Roasted Salmon (see page 62) or Tepsi Kebap (see page 84).

Butternut borani

Very few Persian meals are enjoyed without yogurt in some shape or form, and the most popular dishes are yogurt with cucumber, spinach or Persian wild garlic (which is different to the leafy wild garlic or ramsons found in woodland). When a student once came to my cookery class and told me that the region where her family are from use squash to make a yogurt dish, I had to try it for myself – it is insanely delicious and always the first item to be finished whenever I serve it, with people often being surprised that it's made from butternut squash.

SERVES 4—6

1.2kg butternut squash

olive oil, for drizzling

2 garlic cloves, minced

300g Greek yogurt

½ small packet (about 15g) of dill, very finely chopped

1 teaspoon pul biber chilli flakes

handful of walnut pieces

Maldon sea salt flakes and freshly ground black pepper

flatbread, to serve

Preheat the oven to 220°C (200°C fan), Gas Mark 7. Line a baking tray with baking paper.

Leaving the skin on, cut the butternut squash in half lengthways and, using a spoon, scoop out the seeds and discard. Place the squash halves cut side up on the prepared baking tray and rub the exposed flesh with a little drizzle of olive oil. Roast for about 45–50 minutes, then insert a knife into the thickest part of the flesh to check if it's soft and cooked through. If or when the squash is cooked, remove from the oven and leave until cool enough to handle.

Using a spoon, scoop all the squash flesh out of the skins into a mixing bowl, then mash as best as you can. Add the garlic, a drizzle of olive oil and a generous amount of salt and pepper, followed by the yogurt, and give everything a good stir. Check and adjust the seasoning, then transfer the borani on to a plate, spread it right to the edges and smooth over with the back of the spoon. Drizzle with olive oil and scatter over the pul biber, dill and, finally, the walnuts before serving with flatbread.

SIMPLY DELICIOUS WITH...

Harissa Chicken Noodle Lettuce Cups (see page 115) or Sticky Harissa, Sesame & Pistachio Chicken (see page 147).

Green hummus

This is a very different hummus flavour-wise from the traditional variety. I really love the vibrant colour but the punchy combination of herbs also gives it a unique flavour that pairs really well with crudités, lettuce leaves and pitta bread. It's also perfect as a filling for sandwiches and wraps. Mostly, though, I like to dip raw carrots into it, as the sweetness works really well, but then again, for a girl like me, hummus can always be eaten on its own by the heaped spoonful.

SERVES 6–8

2 x 400g cans chickpeas, drained and
¾ of the brine of 1 can reserved
juice of ½ lemon, or more to taste
2 garlic cloves, peeled
1 small packet (about 30g) of flat leaf
parsley
1 small packet (about 30g) of fresh
coriander
½ small packet (about 15g) of
tarragon, leaves picked

2 tablespoons tahini
generous amount of Maldon sea salt
flakes and freshly ground black
pepper
pitta bread, to serve

TO GARNISH
1 teaspoon nigella seeds
olive oil

Put all the main ingredients into a blender (if using a food processor, you will need to mince the garlic and roughly chop the herbs first) and blitz until smooth.

Check and adjust the seasoning, adding more lemon juice to taste. Serve garnished with the nigella seeds and a drizzle of olive oil.

SIMPLY DELICIOUS WITH...

Fragrant Fish Cakes with Preserved Lemon Mayonnaise (see page 152) or Crispy Prawns with a Mango & Tomato Dip (see page 164).

Lamb & mint kofte

These simple yet delicious little kofte are based on something I tasted in a restaurant in Antakya (the Ancient Roman city of Antioch in southern Turkey), and use dried mint – a wonderfully versatile ingredient. These kofte really are pleasingly straightforward and a recipe that I've made many times since coming back from that trip.

MAKES ABOUT 20

500g minced lamb

1 onion, minced in a food processor and drained of any liquid, or very finely chopped

2 tablespoons dried mint

2 eggs

vegetable oil, for frying

generous amount of Maldon sea salt flakes and freshly ground black pepper

TO SERVE

Greek or natural yogurt

chopped fresh mint leaves

Put all the main ingredients, except the vegetable oil, into a large mixing bowl and, using your hands, work them together really well, pummelling the meat mixture for several minutes into a smooth, even paste.

Take golf-ball-sized amounts of the mixture and shape into round patties, about 20 in total.

Heat a large frying pan over a medium-high heat. Once hot, drizzle in a little vegetable oil and cook the patties in batches for 3–4 minutes on each side until browned on both sides and cooked through. Thread each patty on to a little wooden skewer and serve with a bowl of Greek or natural yogurt scattered with some chopped fresh mint for dipping.

SIMPLY DELICIOUS WITH...

Flame-roasted Pepper, Pistachio & Dill Yogurt (see page 42) or Maast-o-Esfenaj (see page 72).

TIP

Keep the first batch of patties warm covered in foil while you cook the second batch, then reheat them in the pan if necessary.

Ultimate falafels

These falafel are less traditional and more Sabrina style – packed with herbs and bolstered with extra flavour – but the results are every bit as satisfying.

MAKES 20—25

250g dried chickpeas

50g flat leaf parsley, roughly chopped

50g fresh coriander, roughly chopped

1 large carrot, scrubbed and grated

2 large garlic cloves, very finely
chopped

4 fat spring onions, very thinly sliced

1 onion, very finely chopped

2 tablespoons plain flour

1 teaspoon baking powder

1 tablespoon ground coriander

1 teaspoon ground turmeric

vegetable oil, for deep-frying

Maldon sea salt flakes and freshly
ground black pepper

TO SERVE

pitta breads, sliced gherkins, sliced
tomatoes, sliced red cabbage,
Greek or natural yogurt (or vegan
alternative), chilli sauce

Soak the chickpeas in cold water overnight, or for 8–10 hours, then drain.

Put the chickpeas along with all the remaining main ingredients, except the vegetable oil, into a food processor and season generously with salt and pepper. Blitz until evenly combined but still slightly coarse in texture (don't worry too much about the consistency).

Pour enough oil into a deep frying pan or saucepan to fill to a depth of about 4cm. Heat the oil over a medium heat and bring to frying temperature – it should be hot but not smoking (add a pinch of mixture: if it sizzles immediately, the oil is hot enough). Line a plate with kitchen paper.

Take scoops of the mixture and roll into smooth balls about 4cm in diameter. Fry the falafels in batches, a few at a time without overcrowding the pan, for 2–3 minutes, or until just starting to brown all over. Remove with a slotted spoon and transfer to the paper-lined plate to drain. Serve hot in pitta breads with pickled cucumbers, tomatoes, Greek yogurt and chilli sauce.

SIMPLY DELICIOUS WITH...

Thyme & Za'atar Roasted Tomatoes with Strained Yogurt Balls (see page 11).

TIP
You really need dried chickpeas for this recipe – don't be tempted
to substitute the canned variety as they will result in mushy falafels.

Kabab koobideh

For Persians, this dish is an institution. The word 'kebab' (or *kabab*, as Persians call it) means 'to grill', usually over fire. The first kebabs were made by Persian soldiers who would grill meats on their swords, hence the traditional flat, sword-like skewers Persians use today – you can buy them online if you want to serve them this way. Although we only have a few different varieties of kebab, for me, this is simplest yet most delicious.

MAKES 5–6 LARGE KEBABS OR 10–12 SMALL PATTIES

1kg minced lamb (30% fat is essential)

2 large onions, minced in a food processor and drained of any liquid, or very finely chopped

2 level tablespoons ground turmeric

2 level teaspoons bicarbonate of soda

Maldon sea salt flakes and freshly ground black pepper

6 tomatoes

flatbreads, to serve

Put all the main ingredients into a large mixing bowl and, using your hands, work them together really well, pummelling the meat mixture for several minutes into a smooth paste.

To make large kebabs, divide the mixture into 5–6 portions and form each portion around a flat sword skewer about 25cm long. Using your thumb and forefinger, pinch the meat widthways from one end of the kebab to the other to create the classic ridges. Cook them over a charcoal barbecue that has been burning for about 30 minutes, alongside the whole tomatoes. The trick is to cook them for about 10–15 minutes in total until the meat is browned and cooked through, while turning them every 2 minutes to help the fat render and to prevent them burning – if they start to burn, your barbecue is too hot.

To make small kebabs, preheat your oven to its highest setting (with fan if it has one). Line a large baking tray with baking paper. Divide the mixture into 10–12 portions, form into sausages, then flatten and pinch as above to create ridges. Place on the prepared baking tray with the tomatoes and bake for 10–12 minutes.

Serve the kebabs and tomatoes immediately on flatbreads so the bread absorbs the lovely juices.

SIMPLY DELICIOUS WITH... Naan-o-Paneer-o-Sabzi (see page 108)

TIP
This recipe only works if you use minced meat containing 30 per cent fat or more – it plays a vital part in keeping the kebab juicy and bursting with flavour.

Tepsi kebap

What the Turks don't know about making kebabs just isn't worth knowing. *Tepsi* is the Turkish word for 'tray', which is what this recipe is traditionally cooked in, and *kebap* is the Turkish word for 'kebab'. I visited a butcher's shop attached to a restaurant in Antakya in Turkey and was roped into hand-mincing the ingredients for this particular recipe using a giant machete-like knife. The mixture was then pressed into a baking tray and baked in a wood-fired oven. The results were spectacular, and the flavour was so memorable that I came back home and created a version in a shallow casserole. If any one recipe changes the way you cook, this may just be it – the meat is juicy, tender and charred on top, and the ease of pressing the meat into the dish makes this a super-simple way to make a kebab.

SERVES 4–6

500g minced lamb (20% fat)

1 onion, minced in a food processor and drained of any liquid, or very finely chopped

2 large garlic cloves, minced

½ red pepper, cored, deseeded and very finely chopped

50g flat leaf parsley, leaves and stalks finely chopped, plus extra leaves to serve

2 tablespoons tomato purée

1 tablespoon pul biber chilli flakes

½ teaspoon bicarbonate of soda

generous amount of Maldon sea salt flakes and freshly ground black pepper

TO SERVE

tortilla wraps or bread

sliced red onion

Greek yogurt, optional

Preheat your oven to its highest setting. Select an ovenproof dish or baking tray – I use a shallow cast-iron casserole dish about 22cm in diameter.

Put all the main ingredients into a large mixing bowl and, using your hands, work them together well, pummelling the meat mixture for several minutes into a smooth, even paste.

Press the meat mixture into the ovenproof dish or baking tray to cover the base and bake for 18 minutes, or until golden on top. Serve immediately with tortilla wraps or bread, some sliced red onion, parsley leaves and Greek yogurt, if liked.

SIMPLY DELICIOUS WITH...

Tomato & Garlic Rice (see page 38) or Maast-o-Esfenaj (see page 72).

Tahchin

Forced by my mother to learn and perfect *tahchin*, I finally achieved a version that I think retains the authentic qualities of this classic baked rice cake while paring it down to make it achievable for anyone who wants to give it a go. Barberries are key to this recipe and Persians love frying these sour little berries in butter and sugar to create a layer in the centre and sometimes garnish the top with a generous quantity, too. I've kept this recipe simple by sticking to the middle layer only, which gives the most wonderfully sharp yet sweet and fruity tang sandwiched between two layers of saffron-scented rice. In essence, this dish is truly spectacular and a comforting family favourite of mine.

SERVES 6—8

500g basmati rice

olive oil, for frying

1 large onion, halved and thinly sliced
    into half moons

500g boneless, skinless chicken thighs,
    cut into 1cm cubes

100g butter

300g Greek yogurt

1g (about a pinch) saffron threads,
    ground to a powder using a pestle
    and mortar, then steeped in
    5 tablespoons boiling water until cool

3 eggs

150g dried barberries

50g caster sugar

melted ghee or vegetable oil, for oiling

Maldon sea salt flakes and freshly
    ground black pepper

Bring a large saucepan of water to the boil. Add the rice and stir to avoid the grains from sticking together, then parboil for about 6–7 minutes until the grains turn from a dullish off-white colour to a more opaque, brilliant white and have slightly elongated – they should still remain firm to the bite. Drain and immediately rinse thoroughly under cold running water, running your fingers through the rice, until all the grains are well rinsed of starch and completely cooled. Drain the rice thoroughly by shaking the sieve well, then leave for any remaining water to drain. Shake off any excess water before use.

CONTINUED OVERLEAF

Place a small saucepan over a medium heat, drizzle in a little olive oil and add the onion. Cook for a few minutes until softened and translucent. Add the chicken and mix into the onion, then cook over a gentle heat for 30 minutes until cooked through and tender.

Preheat the oven to 200°C (180°C fan), Gas Mark 6.

Once the chicken is cooked, add half the butter, and as soon as it melts, remove the pan from the heat and mix through. Transfer the contents of the pan to a large mixing bowl, add the parboiled rice, yogurt, saffron solution and eggs and mix thoroughly until evenly combined. Season generously with salt and pepper and mix again.

Place a frying pan over a medium heat and add the remaining 50g butter. Once it has melted, add the barberries and then the sugar. Stir to coat the barberries in the sugar and butter mixture, then as soon as the sugar dissolves, immediately remove the pan from the heat, or the sugar will crystallize.

Line a 32 x 22cm ovenproof dish with baking paper and brush with melted ghee or vegetable oil (if using a nonstick dish, just brush with melted ghee or oil). Pour half the rice mixture into the dish and shake it to compress the rice and ensure it is in an even layer. Scatter the barberries on top to coat the surface and pour over the remaining rice mixture. Smooth the surface and bake on the lowest shelf in the oven for 1 hour 20–30 minutes until the edges start to brown.

Once cooked, place a tray or platter over the dish and carefully flip the tahchin on to the tray or platter, then serve immediately.

SIMPLY DELICIOUS WITH...

Green-yogurt-dressed Baby Gem Lettuce with Burnt Hazelnuts (see page 44) or Maast-o-Esfenaj (see page 72).

Albaloo polow

This classic Persian rice dish of lamb and sour cherry meatballs best showcases our long-standing historic culinary tradition of combining meat with fruits. Try it with beef mince instead of lamb, and substitute sweetened cranberries if you can't find sour cherries. You can also leave out the meatballs completely and serve the polow with a roast chicken or just on its own, but the meatballs were my favourite bit as a child.

SERVES 6—8

500g minced lamb (20% fat)

1 onion, minced in a food processor and drained of any liquid, or very finely chopped

1 tablespoon garlic granules

vegetable oil, for frying

500g basmati rice

400ml boiling water

400g sweetened dried Morello or sour cherries (or use sweetened dried cranberries)

2 tablespoons ghee

Maldon sea salt flakes and freshly ground black pepper

Put the minced lamb, onion, garlic granules and a generous amount of salt and pepper into a mixing bowl and, using your hands, work the ingredients together really well, pummelling the meat mixture for several minutes into a smooth, even paste. Roll the mixture into balls 2cm in diameter – about 40 in total.

Heat a large frying pan over a high heat. Line a plate with a double layer of kitchen paper. Once the pan is hot, drizzle in a little vegetable oil and fry the meatballs in 2 batches until all are nicely browned all over. Remove from the pan with a slotted spoon and transfer to the paper-lined plate to drain.

Bring a large, ideally nonstick, saucepan of salted water to the boil. Add the rice and stir to avoid the grains from sticking together, then parboil for about 6–7 minutes until the grains turn from a dullish off-white colour to a more opaque, brilliant white and have slightly elongated. Drain and immediately rinse thoroughly under cold running water, running your fingers through the rice, until all the grains are well rinsed of starch and completely cooled. Drain the rice thoroughly by shaking the sieve well, then leave for 5–10 minutes for any remaining water to drain. Shake off any excess water before use.

CONTINUED OVERLEAF

Meanwhile, pour the boiling water into a small saucepan and place over a medium heat. Add the sour cherries and boil, stirring frequently, for several minutes until the mixture reduces, turns syrupy and coats the back of a spoon (see Tip).

Rinse the rice saucepan and place over a gentle heat. (If the pan isn't nonstick, first line the base with a large square of baking paper – see Tip on page 102.) Add the ghee, and once melted, pour in enough cold water to come 1cm up the side of the pan. Swirl the pan around to mix the ghee and water together, then add a generous amount of crushed salt flakes. Loosely scatter just enough rice into the pan to coat the base in an even layer (don't pack the mixture into the pan), then mix the rest of the rice with the cherries and meatballs until evenly combined. Scatter (do not press) the rice mixture into the pan, allowing for natural air pockets, and smooth out to the sides. Using the handle of a wooden spoon, poke a series of holes into the rice, piercing all the way to the base of the pan (this allows the steam to circulate).

Wrap the pan lid in a clean tea towel so that it fits tightly on the pan. If using a gas hob, cook over the lowest flame for 1 hour. If using an electric/induction hob, cook over a medium heat for 20 minutes, then reduce the heat to medium-low and cook for a further 1½–2 hours.

Once cooked, remove the lid and smooth the rice over to the edges to create a flat base. Place a large platter over the pan and carefully flip the polow on to the platter to reveal the crispy *tahdig* base. Don't be disheartened by the dark crust; this is due to the dark cherry juice, which is also sweet so has a tendency to caramelize and as a result sometimes appears blackened, even though it may not actually be burned.

SIMPLY DELICIOUS WITH...

Maast-o-Esfenaj (see page 72) or Cucumber, Green Apple & Nigella Salad with Feta & Dill (see page 48).

TIP

If your cherries have too much liquid around them, boil until reduced, otherwise they will make the rice too wet and the juice will seep to the base and burn the crust.

Tahdig e Makaroni

This is an absolute classic Persian dish; the pasta is given the same *tahdig* (crispy base)
treatment as our rice dishes, and the crust is chewy, crunchy and out of this world.
Not remotely Italian, but a much-loved Persian staple that you need to try at least once.

SERVES 6

500g spaghetti

olive oil, for frying

1 large onion, very finely chopped

500g minced beef

1 heaped teaspoon ground turmeric

1 heaped teaspoon garlic granules

140g tomato purée

200ml cold water

1 heaped teaspoon sugar

25g butter

2 tablespoons ghee or vegetable oil

Maldon sea salt flakes and black pepper

Cook the spaghetti in a large saucepan of salted boiling water according to the packet
instructions. Drain and rinse under cold running water, then drain again and set aside.

Place a large frying pan over a medium heat and pour in enough olive oil to coat the base of
the pan. Add the onion and cook for a few minutes until beginning to brown, then add the
minced beef and mix with the onion. Stir in the turmeric, garlic granules, tomato purée and
a generous amount of salt and pepper (the mixture will need over-seasoning at this stage).

Increase the heat and cook until the meat browns, then add the cold water and sugar and mix
well. Cook until most of the water has evaporated, stirring occasionally to prevent sticking,
then remove from the heat. Stir in the butter to create a glossy sauce, then set aside.

Place a nonstick saucepan over a gentle heat. (If your pan isn't nonstick, first line the base with
a square of baking paper – see Tip on page 102.) Add the ghee or oil and season the base with
salt. Once the ghee has melted, pour in enough cold water to come 1cm up the side of the pan.
Swirl the pan around to mix the ghee and water together. Add 2 handfuls of the cooked
spaghetti to the pan to cover the base generously. Mix the remaining spaghetti with the meat
sauce, then pour it all into the pan and cover with a lid.

If using a gas hob, cook over the lowest flame for 1 hour. If using an electric/induction hob,
cook over a medium heat for 20 minutes, then reduce the heat to medium-low and cook for
a further 1½ hours.

Once cooked, remove the lid, place a large platter over the pan and carefully flip the makaroni
on to the platter to serve. No accompaniment needed.

Maman Malek's Borscht

You may be surprised to hear that this is my grandmother's recipe, especially since she spent so little time cooking when I was a child. She absolutely hated being in the kitchen, but once in a blue moon she would prepare a meal and borscht was one among her limited repertoire. We Persians do have some Russian-influenced dishes in our cuisine. Of course, our versions may be wildly different from the original recipes, but they have cemented my love for all kinds of Russian dishes today.

SERVES 4–6

3 tablespoons vegetable oil

2 small onions, halved and sliced into thin half moons

600g bone-in beef shin (about 2 steaks)

3–4 small oxtail pieces (about 250g total weight)

1 heaped teaspoon coriander seeds

500g red beetroot, scrubbed and grated

350g red cabbage, finely shredded

Maldon sea salt flakes and freshly ground black pepper

TO SERVE

100g Greek or natural yogurt

½ small packet (about 15g) of dill, chopped, optional

Place a large saucepan over a medium heat and pour in the vegetable oil. Add the onions and cook for a few minutes until softened and translucent, then add the beef shin steaks, the oxtail, a very generous amount of pepper (about 1 tablespoon) and the coriander seeds and stir until the meat is well coated in the onions and spices. Seal the meat on both sides but without letting it brown.

Add the beetroot and cabbage, pour over enough cold water to cover all the ingredients and season generously with salt. Stir well, then reduce the heat to medium-low and gently simmer for 30 minutes.

Skim the scum from the surface of the borscht and continue to cook uncovered for another 30 minutes, then cover with a lid and simmer for a further 3½–4½ hours until the meat is tender and falls apart – remove the lid for the final 30 minutes of cooking time. Serve with the Greek or natural yogurt and dill.

Turmeric & black pepper braised lamb neck

Persians traditionally make this recipe as an accompaniment to a broad bean and dill rice dish, but they usually use lamb shanks. I do love lamb shanks but they can be quite expensive and aren't always easy to find. I taught this version of a classic recipe at my cookery classes and was surprised by how much people loved it and treated it more like a stew, so much so that I decided it was high time I shared it with you.

SERVES 6

vegetable oil, for frying

2 large onions, halved and thinly
    sliced into half moons

4 fat garlic cloves, bashed and thinly
    sliced

800g lamb neck fillets, cut into
    2.5cm chunks

2 heaped teaspoons ground turmeric

1 heaped teaspoon coarsely ground
    black pepper

2 heaped teaspoons Maldon sea salt
    flakes, crushed

rice, to serve

Place a large saucepan over a medium-high heat and pour in enough vegetable oil to coat the base of the pan. Add the onions and cook for a few minutes until softened and translucent, without colouring, then stir in the garlic and cook for a few minutes.

Add the lamb, turmeric and pepper and stir until the chunks of meat are well coated in the onion mixture. Seal the meat on all sides but without browning.

Add the salt, then pour in enough boiling water to just about cover the contents of the pan, cover the pan with a lid, reduce the heat to low and simmer gently for 2½ hours. Check the pan every so often, giving the contents a stir and checking on the liquid level to ensure there is always just enough to barely cover the meat but also so that the sauce thickens a little and eventually reduces. About 30 minutes before the end of the cooking time, taste the sauce and season with more salt if necessary. Serve with rice.

SIMPLY DELICIOUS WITH...

Adas Polow (see page 101) or Polow-e Bademjan-o-Felfel (see page 125).

Koofteh berenji

I'm told this dish of lamb, rice and yellow split-pea meatballs was my Grandpa Baba Ghayour's favourite thing to eat. He passed away when I was two, so this is one of my ways to remember him and keep his memory alive. My grandmother, who absolutely hated cooking, learned to make these knowing how much he loved them – if that's not love, then I don't know what is. This is the dish you want to come home to on a cold night and is also perfect for batch freezing once cooked. You can also make them whatever size you fancy, big or small.

SERVES 6

150g yellow split peas

150g basmati rice

500g minced lamb (20% fat)

1 small packet (about 30g) of flat leaf parsley, finely chopped

1 small packet (about 30g) of dill, finely chopped

1 small packet (about 30g) of chives, finely chopped

1 small packet (about 30g) of fresh coriander, finely chopped

2 tablespoons plain flour

3 teaspoons ground turmeric

generous pinch of saffron threads, ground to a powder using a pestle and mortar, then steeped in 3 tablespoons boiling water until cool

4 garlic cloves, minced

2 large onions, 1 minced in a food processor and drained of any liquid, or very finely chopped, and 1 halved and thinly sliced into half moons

2 handfuls of dried barberries

3 eggs

vegetable oil, for frying

1 heaped tablespoon tomato purée

400g can chopped tomatoes

1 litre boiling water

Maldon sea salt flakes and freshly ground black pepper

TO SERVE
Greek or natural yogurt
flatbreads

Bring a small saucepan of water to the boil and stir in a generous amount of crumbled salt flakes. Add the yellow split peas and stir, then reduce the heat to medium and simmer for 25 minutes until the split peas are cooked. Drain and set aside to cool.

CONTINUED OVERLEAF

Refill the pan with water, bring to the boil and stir in salt as before. Add the rice and stir to avoid the grains sticking together, then parboil for 7 minutes until the grains turn from a dullish off-white colour to a more opaque, brilliant white and have slightly elongated. Drain and set aside to cool.

Put the cooled rice and split peas into a large mixing bowl with the lamb, herbs, flour, 2 teaspoons of the turmeric, the saffron solution, half the garlic, the minced or very finely chopped onion, the barberries, eggs and a generous amount of salt and pepper. Mix together until evenly combined. Divide the mixture into 12 portions and then roll and compress each portion into a smooth ball.

Place a large saucepan over a medium heat and pour in enough vegetable oil to coat the base of the pan. Add the sliced onion and fry gently for a few minutes until it begins to colour slightly. Add the remaining garlic and gently fry for 2–3 minutes, then stir in the tomato purée and the remaining teaspoon of turmeric. Tip in the canned tomatoes, stir until evenly distributed and season with a generous amount of salt and pepper, then pour in the boiling water and stir to mix.

Bring the sauce to a gentle boil and then add each koofteh (meatball), one at a time, to the sauce. Cover the pan with a lid but leave it slightly ajar and simmer for 20 minutes. Using 2 teaspoons, gently turn the meatballs over, then replace the pan lid as before and continue cooking for a further 30–45 minutes. Serve with yogurt and flatbreads.

SIMPLY DELICIOUS WITH...

Maast-o-Esfenaj (see page 72) or Naan-o-Paneer-o-Sabzi (see page 108).

TIP
You can keep the meatballs cooking in the sauce over a low heat for up to 1 hour, but just ensure the sauce doesn't reduce too much – it should be a soup-like consistency rather than a thick sauce.

Adas polow

This is one of the rice dishes that I loved as a child. My mother was never a big fan, but my grandmother absolutely adored it, although she rarely made it herself. Her love for it was infectious and so, later in life, I taught myself how to make it and began teaching it at my cookery classes with great success. Some people like to add chopped dates, but I find the combination of raisins, lentils and saffron to be the perfect balance.

SERVES 6—8

200g uncooked green lentils
500g basmati rice
2 tablespoons ghee
2–3 generous handfuls of raisins, to taste
2 pinches of saffron threads,
    finely crumbled
75g salted butter, cut into small cubes
Maldon sea salt flakes

Parboil the lentils in a saucepan of salted boiling water for 15 minutes. Drain and rinse thoroughly under cold running water until cold, then drain again and set aside.

Bring a large, ideally nonstick, saucepan of salted water to the boil and stir in a generous handful of crumbled salt flakes. Add the rice and stir to avoid the grains from sticking together, then parboil for about 6–7 minutes until the grains turn from a dullish off-white colour to a more opaque, brilliant white and have slightly elongated. Drain and immediately rinse thoroughly under cold running water, running your fingers through the rice, until all the grains are well rinsed of starch and completely cooled. Drain the rice thoroughly by shaking the sieve well, then leave for 5–10 minutes for any remaining water to drain. Shake off any excess water before use, then tip into a large mixing bowl.

Rinse the saucepan and place over a gentle heat. (If the pan isn't nonstick, first line the base with a large square of baking paper – see Tip overleaf.) Add the ghee, and once melted, pour in enough cold water to come 1cm up the side of the pan. Swirl the pan around to mix the ghee and water together, then add a generous amount of crushed salt flakes.

CONTINUED OVERLEAF

Loosely scatter just enough rice into the pan to coat the base in an even layer (don't pack the mixture into the pan). Mix the raisins, lentils and crumbled saffron into the remaining rice until evenly combined. Scatter (do not press) the rice mixture into the pan, allowing for natural air pockets, and smooth out to the sides. Using the handle of a wooden spoon, poke a series of holes into the rice, piercing all the way to the base of the pan (this allows the steam to circulate), then dot the cubes of butter over the surface.

Wrap the pan lid in a clean tea towel so that it fits tightly on the pan. If using a gas hob, cook over the lowest flame for 1 hour. If using an electric/induction hob, cook over a medium heat for 20 minutes, then reduce the heat to medium-low and cook for a further 1½–2 hours.

Once cooked, remove the lid and smooth the rice over to the edges to create a flat base. Place a large serving dish over the pan and carefully flip the polow on to the dish to reveal the crunchy *tahdig* base. Alternatively, spoon out the rice, then scrape out the *tahdig* base and serve it on top of the rice. Just remember that the raisins contain sugar, so any that caught on the bottom of the pan may appear blackened, which is absolutely fine.

SIMPLY DELICIOUS WITH...

Spice-rubbed Spatchcocked Poussin (see page 55).

TIP
If you scrunch up the square of baking paper and then smooth it out, this makes it more flexible and therefore easier to line the pan with.

Khoresh-e-karafs

This lamb, celery and herb stew is one of my absolute favourite Persian *khoresh* (stew) recipes, and one I teach regularly at my Persian cookery classes. In this, the celery is tender, almost soft, and packed full of the fragrant dried mint, parsley and citrus-spiked meat broth. It freezes beautifully, so make things easy, double the batch and freeze the rest for a rainy day – you won't regret it.

SERVES 6—8

vegetable oil, for frying

1 head of celery, sticks separated and cut into 3cm lengths

2 white onions, diced

800g lamb neck fillet, cut widthways into 2cm-thick pieces

2 teaspoons ground turmeric

3 heaped tablespoons dried mint

200g flat leaf parsley, roughly chopped

juice of ½ lemon, or more to taste

Maldon sea salt flakes and freshly ground black pepper

basmati rice, to serve

Heat your largest saucepan over a medium heat. Pour in enough vegetable oil to generously coat the base of the pan. Add the celery and cook for 20–30 minutes, stirring occasionally, until completely soft, without browning. The celery should lose its colour and turn grey when cooked. Remove the celery with a slotted spoon and set aside. Return the pan to the heat, add the onions and leave to sweat in the leftover oil for a few minutes until softened and translucent, without browning. It's important not to brown the vegetables (or the meat, for that matter), as we don't want any brown colouring in this dish.

Add the lamb pieces and stir to coat them in the onion mixture, then add the turmeric and dried mint and mix well until the meat is evenly coated. Next, add the parsley, and this is where you need to pay special attention. Cook for 20–30 minutes, stirring regularly and without browning the parsley, until it has completely wilted, reduced in volume, lost its bright colour and has the appearence of very well-cooked spinach – this step is integral to the success of this dish.

Return the cooked celery to the pan and fold into the meat and herb mixture as best you can. Add the lemon juice and a generous amount of salt and pepper and mix well, then pour over enough boiling water to barely cover the ingredients. Cover the pan with a lid, reduce the heat to low and cook for 1 hour, stirring occasionally.

Remove the lid and check and adjust the seasoning to taste, then cook, uncovered, for a further hour or so until the meat is tender before serving with plain basmati rice.

Spicy bulgur wheat meatballs
in garlicky tomato sauce

I once travelled to the Cappadocia region of Anatolia in central Turkey to visit the famous ancient rock formations, and during that trip I fell in love with this recipe – *sulu köfte*: tiny little meatballs containing bulgur wheat, so this is my homage to that recipe. Traditionally, they are served as a soup or with a locally made pasta called *eriste*, but tagliatelle works beautifully.

SERVES 6–8 (MAKES ABOUT 45 MEATBALLS)

500g minced lamb (20% fat)

100g uncooked bulgur wheat

1 large onion, minced in a food
    processor or very finely chopped

1 tablespoon dried oregano

1 tablespoon garlic granules

1 teaspoon ground turmeric

1 teaspoon paprika

Maldon sea salt flakes and freshly
    ground black pepper

cooked, buttered tagliatelle, to serve

FOR THE SAUCE

3–4 tablespoons olive oil

1 large head of garlic, cloves separated
    and thinly sliced

2 x 400g cans chopped tomatoes

500ml cold water

½–1 teaspoon chilli flakes, to taste

Maldon sea salt flakes and freshly
    ground black pepper

Put all the main ingredients into a large mixing bowl and, using your hands, work them together really well for a few minutes until evenly combined. Roll the mixture into 4cm balls, compressing the mixture firmly to ensure they retain their shape.

To make the sauce, place a large saucepan over a medium heat and drizzle in the olive oil. Add the garlic and cook for a few minutes until translucent, without browning. Add the canned tomatoes, chilli flakes, the water and a generous amount of salt and pepper.

Bring the sauce to a gentle boil, add the meatballs and stir to coat in the sauce, then simmer gently for about 1 hour or so with a lid on but slightly ajar until the meatballs are cooked through. You want to reduce the liquid to a rich sauce-like consistency so remove the lid after 30 minutes if it looks too watery. Check and adjust the seasoning before serving with buttered tagliatelle.

SIMPLY DELICIOUS WITH…

Flame-roasted Pepper, Pistachio & Dill Yogurt (see page 42).

Naan-o-paneer-o-sabzi
Persian cheese platter

I know what you're thinking – a cheese platter? But if you want to know what Persians eat, from the banquets of royal palaces and lavish weddings down to the humblest of family meals, this dish is always there, all year round. Naan-o-paneer-o-sabzi (bread, cheese, herbs) we call it – the ubiquitous sharing plate served at the beginning of a meal but always on the table throughout. It really is stunningly simple and particularly useful to serve to guests to buy you some time in the kitchen if you are running a little behind with the cooking.

SERVES 4

16 radishes
8 spring onions
generous handful of walnut halves
200g block of vegetarian feta cheese
4 sprigs of tarragon
generous handful of mint leaves
generous handful of basil leaves
flatbreads or tortilla wraps, quartered, to serve

Using a small sharp knife, cut a deep cross in the top of each radish running down close to the base, then plunge into a bowl of cold water. Trim the ends of the green parts of the spring onions then trim the bulb end. Starting at the bulb end, cut a deep cross running halfway down the length of each spring onion. Plunge into the bowl of cold water with the radishes. Leave to soak for about 1 hour.

Meanwhile, soak the walnuts in hot water from the tap for about 1 hour.

Once the soaking time has elapsed, select a large wooden platter or chopping board and place the feta on it. Drain and rinse the walnuts, then drain them again and dry on kitchen paper. Drain the radishes and spring onions and dry them on kitchen paper, too.

Arrange the herbs, walnuts, radishes and spring onions on the platter or board, then serve with flatbreads.

SIMPLY DELICIOUS WITH...
Kabab Koobideh (see page 82) and Tepsi Kebap (see page 84).

The melting pot

Courgette & oregano pancakes
with feta & honey

Courgettes are so versatile, and I absolutely love the Turkish take on them in the form of courgette and feta fritters called *mücver*. Taking inspiration from them, these pancakes make for a wonderful breakfast or brunch dish, topped with creamy, salty feta and a good drizzle of sweet honey – my idea of perfection.

MAKES ABOUT 16

2 large courgettes

2 eggs

4 tablespoons plain flour

1 teaspoon baking powder

½ small packet (about 15g) of
    oregano, leaves finely chopped

1 teaspoon cumin seeds

1 heaped teaspoon pul biber chilli
    flakes, plus extra to serve

vegetable oil, for frying

Maldon sea salt flakes and freshly
    ground black pepper

TO SERVE

100g vegetarian feta cheese, crumbled

clear honey

Coarsely grate the courgettes into a bowl. Tip them into a clean tea towel, gather up the sides and squeeze out the liquid from the courgettes. Place in a mixing bowl, add the eggs, flour, baking powder, oregano, cumin and pul biber, season generously with salt and pepper and beat together.

Place a large frying pan over a medium-high heat and drizzle in some vegetable oil. Using a tablespoon measure, roughly fill the scoop with the courgette mixture and without overcrowding add dollops to the pan, then gently flatten. Fry for about 1 minute until the undersides are nicely browned, then flip over and cook until the other sides have browned. Remove from the pan and repeat with the remaining mixture.

Serve the pancakes immediately topped with the crumbled feta, a little drizzle of honey and a sprinkling of pul biber.

SIMPLY DELICIOUS WITH...

Roasted Nectarines with Labneh, Herbs & Honey (see page 69).

Harissa chicken noodle lettuce cups

Lettuce cups are one of my favourite things to eat – I'll pile them high with flavourful fillings and munch on them at any opportunity. This combo of sweet and spicy noodles with shredded chicken is a great one for sharing and especially perfect in the warmer months (although I never let a thing like weather dictate when I eat these) – a perfectly virtuous snack, finger food or main meal.

SERVES 4—6

2 boneless, skinless chicken breasts

75g rice vermicelli noodles, cooked according to the packet instructions and rinsed until cold

75g fine green beans, thinly sliced

4 spring onions, thinly sliced from root to tip

1 carrot, peeled, cut lengthways into thirds and then into matchsticks

1 small packet (about 30g) of fresh coriander, finely chopped

3 heads of Baby Gem lettuce, leaves carefully separated

Maldon sea salt flakes and freshly ground black pepper

FOR THE DRESSING

2 tablespoons clear honey

1 heaped tablespoon rose harissa

1 tablespoon soy sauce

1 tablespoon olive oil

finely grated zest and juice of 1 unwaxed lime

1 heaped teaspoon nigella seeds

Maldon sea salt flakes

Bring a saucepan of water to a gentle boil, add the chicken breasts and poach for 8–10 minutes, or until the juices run clear when the thickest part of the meat is pierced with the tip of a sharp knife.

Remove the chicken with a slotted spoon and leave to cool. Shred the meat and then roughly chop.

Mix all the dressing ingredients together in a jug or small bowl.

Reserve 2 tablespoons of the dressing, then add everything, except the lettuce, to a mixing bowl. Season with salt and pepper and mix together well.

Lay the lettuce leaves on a serving platter. Divide the chicken noodle mixture between the lettuce leaves and serve drizzled with the reserved dressing.

SIMPLY DELICIOUS WITH...

Tomato & Peanut Salad with Tamarind, Ginger & Honey Dressing (see page 137) or Crispy Prawns with a Mango & Tomato Dip (see page 164).

Harissa & lime chicken wings

Sweet, spicy, citrusy, barbecued, Asian – you name it, I have love for all chicken wing recipes. I know what you're thinking looking at the ingredients below… 'fish sauce?!', but trust me, this is inspired by Thai fish sauce chicken wings, which are crispy, salty and incredibly delicious. Of course, I have come up with my own version that is the kind of comforting, finger-lickin' food that should really be made in double portions.

SERVES 4–6

vegetable oil, for deep-frying

1kg chicken wings

FOR THE SAUCE

3 tablespoons fish sauce

3 tablespoons clear honey

2 tablespoons rose harissa

finely grated zest of 1 unwaxed lime
    and juice of ½

Mix all the sauce ingredients together in a large mixing bowl and set aside.

Pour enough oil into a saucepan or deep frying pan to fill to a depth of about 7cm. Heat the oil over a medium-high heat and bring to frying temperature (about 210°C – carefully dip a chicken wing into the oil: if it sizzles immediately, the oil is hot enough, but if it bubbles ferociously, then the oil is too hot, so reduce the heat before you begin cooking). Line a plate with a double layer of kitchen paper.

When the oil is ready for frying, carefully add the chicken wings to the oil and stir briefly to prevent sticking. Deep-fry the chicken for 20–25 minutes, or until crispy and golden brown and cooked through – you may need to do this in 2 batches. Remove the chicken from the oil with a slotted spoon and transfer to the paper-lined plate to drain. Keep the first batch warm under foil while you cook the second batch.

While still hot, add the chicken wings to the sauce and toss until well coated, then serve immediately.

SIMPLY DELICIOUS WITH…

Baked Sweet Potato, Za'atar & Garlic Chips (see page 34).

Lamb, cumin, coriander & chilli kebabs

My local Pakistani restaurant has always made the most insanely delicious lamb kebabs, and while this recipe is very different, it is inspired by their fiery and aromatic creation, and I have simplified it to suit home cooking using a griddle pan on the hob. These are a delicious delight and perfect with a little cooling yogurt on the side.

MAKES 6

500g minced lamb (20% fat)

1 onion, minced in a food processor and drained of any liquid, or very finely chopped

4 fat garlic cloves, minced

50g fresh coriander, finely chopped

1 tablespoon cumin seeds

1–2 teaspoons chilli flakes, to taste

Maldon sea salt flakes and freshly ground black pepper

pul biber chilli flakes, to garnish

TO SERVE

rice or flatbreads

Greek or natural yogurt

Put all the main ingredients into a large mixing bowl and, using your hands, work them together really well, pummelling the meat mixture for several minutes into a smooth paste.

Divide the mixture into 6 portions and form each portion into a sausage shape, then thread on to 6 metal or wooden skewers. Roll each sausage on a chopping board to elongate to about 12cm long.

Preheat a nonstick griddle pan over a high heat. Once hot, cook the kebabs for about 8–10 minutes, turning them halfway through the cooking time, until nicely browned on both sides and cooked through.

Sprinkle with pul biber and serve with rice or flatbreads and Greek or natural yogurt.

SIMPLY DELICIOUS WITH...

Butternut Borani (see page 75) or Naan-o-Paneer-o-Sabzi (see page 108).

TIP

Alternatively, cook these kebabs in the oven at its highest fan setting for 12 minutes, or until cooked through and just starting to brown.

Spiced lamb, date, pine nut & feta melts

Initially, I made this filling for pastry cigars at a cookery class of mine a few years back, and when there was a little left over, I took it home to make a quick supper for myself and actually preferred this way of using the mixture. It's really quite indulgent, but again very simple. The sweet, spiced meat mixture works beautifully with the creamy, salty feta and satisfies on every level.

MAKES 8

2 tablespoons vegetable oil

1 large onion, minced in a food processor or very finely chopped

500g minced lamb (20% fat)

3 heaped teaspoons ground cinnamon

2 heaped teaspoons garlic granules

½ teaspoon cayenne pepper

200g dates, pitted and finely chopped

1 small packet (about 30g) of flat leaf parsley, very finely chopped

juice of ¼ lemon

75g pine nuts

3 tablespoons clear honey

8 mini flour tortilla wraps

2 x 200g blocks of feta cheese, crumbled

1 teaspoon pul biber chilli flakes

Maldon sea salt flakes and freshly ground black pepper

Place a large frying pan over a medium-high heat and drizzle in the vegetable oil. Add the onion and cook for a few minutes until soft and golden. Add the minced lamb and immediately begin breaking the meat up as finely as you can to avoid clumps. Turn the heat up to high, add the cinnamon, garlic granules, cayenne and a generous amount of pepper and stir until the meat is well coated in the spices. Continue cooking until the meat is fully cooked.

Remove the pan from the heat and stir in the dates, parsley, lemon juice, pine nuts and honey, then season the mixture with a generous amount of salt, mix well and set aside to cool completely.

Preheat your grill or oven to its highest setting. Line a large baking tray with baking paper and lay the wraps on the tray (you may need to do this in 2 batches). Divide the lamb mixture into 8 equal portions and spread a portion on to each wrap. Sprinkle each generously with crumbled feta and place under the grill or in the oven for 6–7 minutes until the cheese browns. Sprinkle the pul biber on top and serve.

SIMPLY DELICIOUS WITH…

Fennel Salad with Spinach, Cashew & Coriander Seed Dressing (see page 53).

Harissa kofta lettuce cups
with preserved lemon yogurt

These spicy North African-inspired koftas are absolutely addictive, and paired with the citrus yet cooling yogurt, it does become rather impossible to limit yourself to a sensible number. Personally, I like to eat a few as they come, but when I'm really hungry, I will toast and split open a pitta bread and shove a few of the koftas inside for a deeply satisfying snack or meal.

MAKES 10 CUPS

500g minced lamb (20% fat)

3 tablespoons rose harissa

2 large eggs

1 large onion, minced in a food processor and any liquid drained, or very finely chopped

25g flat leaf parsley, very finely chopped

25g fresh coriander, very finely chopped

2 teaspoons ground coriander

2 teaspoons garlic granules

2 teaspoons ground cinnamon

75g pine nuts

vegetable oil

generous amount of Maldon sea salt flakes and freshly ground black pepper

FOR THE PRESERVED LEMON YOGURT

500g Greek yogurt

2 teaspoons dried oregano

1 small packet (about 30g) of mint, leaves stacked, rolled up together and finely sliced widthways into thin ribbons

5–6 small preserved lemons, deseeded and very finely chopped

generous drizzle of olive oil

generous amount of Maldon sea salt flakes and freshly ground black pepper

TO SERVE

about 3 heads of Baby Gem lettuce, leaves carefully separated

3 spring onions, very thinly sliced diagonally from root to tip

1–2 teaspoons pul biber chilli flakes, to taste

CONTINUED OVERLEAF

Mix all the preserved lemon yogurt ingredients together in a small bowl, then set aside.

Put all the main ingredients, except the vegetable oil, into a large mixing bowl and, using your hands, work them together really well, pummelling the meat mixture for several minutes into a smooth paste.

Take golf-ball-sized amounts of the mixture, roll into balls and then elongate into kofta shapes, about 20 in total.

Heat a large frying pan over a medium heat. Once hot, drizzle in a little of the vegetable oil and fry the koftas in batches for 4–5 minutes on each side until they are nicely browned and cooked through. Use a spatula to scrape them out of the pan.

Generously fill as many lettuce leaf 'cups' as you need with the preserved lemon yogurt, then add a kofta or two to each cup, dollop with a little more yogurt and top with the spring onions and a sprinkle of pul biber.

SIMPLY DELICIOUS WITH...

Smoked Aubergine, Tomato, Tamarind, & Peanut Salad (see page 182) or Watermelon, Black Olive & Feta with Cayenne, Honey & Lime Dressing (see page 143).

Polow-e-bademjan-o-felfel

This fried aubergine, pepper and tomato rice isn't a classic Persian dish, but it is very good, and I've made it vegan friendly by using oil instead of butter to ensure no one is left out. I've added sweet red peppers to round this dish off and make it a proper meal, which means there is not much else you need on the side, except maybe a dollop of yogurt or a nice spicy pickle or chutney.

SERVES 6—8

vegetable oil, for frying

3 large aubergines, peeled and cut into
    4cm cubes

2 large onions, roughly chopped

2 red peppers, cored, deseeded
    and diced

1 teaspoon chilli flakes

1 teaspoon black mustard seeds

1 teaspoon cumin seeds

1 teaspoon ground turmeric

3 tablespoons tomato purée

500g basmati rice

Maldon sea salt flakes and freshly
    ground black pepper

Line a large tray with a double layer of kitchen paper. Place a large saucepan over a high heat and pour in enough vegetable oil to fill to a depth of about 2.5cm. Once hot, add the aubergines and stir until well coated in the oil, then cook for about 15 minutes until browned, stirring only occasionally. Remove with a slotted spoon, shaking off any excess oil, then transfer to the paper-lined tray to drain.

Pour off most of the oil from the pan, then return the pan to a medium-high heat, add the onions and cook for a few minutes until softened and translucent, then add the red peppers and cook until softened (but not browned). Next, add the chilli flakes, mustard seeds, cumin seeds, turmeric and tomato purée and stir-fry for 3–4 minutes.

Tip the vegetable mixture into a large mixing bowl, add the aubergines and season with a very generous amount of salt and pepper (the mixture will need over-seasoning at this stage).

Bring a large, ideally nonstick, saucepan of water to the boil. Add the rice and stir to avoid the grains from sticking together, then parboil for about 6–7 minutes until the grains turn from a dullish off-white colour to a more opaque, brilliant white and have slightly elongated.

CONTINUED OVERLEAF

Drain and immediately rinse thoroughly under cold running water, running your fingers through the rice until all the grains are well rinsed of starch and completely cooled. Drain the rice thoroughly by shaking the sieve well, then leave for 5–10 minutes for any remaining water to drain. Shake off any excess water before use.

Rinse the rice saucepan and place over a gentle heat. (If the pan isn't nonstick, first line the base with a large square of baking paper – see Tip on page 102.) Add 4 tablespoons of vegetable oil, then pour in enough cold water to come 1cm up the side of the pan. Swirl the pan around to mix the oil and water together, then add a generous amount of crushed salt flakes. Loosely scatter just enough of the rice into the pan to coat the base in an even layer (don't pack the mixture into the pan), then mix the rest of the rice with the vegetable mixture until evenly combined. Scatter (do not press) the rice mixture into the pan, allowing for natural air pockets, and smooth out to the sides. Using the handle of a wooden spoon, poke a series of holes into the rice, piercing all the way to the base of the pan (this allows the steam to circulate). Wrap the pan lid in a clean tea towel so that it fits tightly on the pan. If using a gas hob, cook over the lowest flame for 1 hour, but if using an electric/induction hob, cook over a medium heat for 20 minutes, then reduce the heat to medium-low and cook for a further 1½–2 hours.

Once cooked, remove the lid and smooth the rice over to the edges to create a flat base. Place a large platter over the pan and carefully flip the polow on to the platter to reveal the crunchy *tahdig* base.

SIMPLY DELICIOUS WITH...

Lamb, Cumin, Coriander & Chilli Kebabs (see page 118) and Pomegranate Molasses & Honey-glazed Meatballs (see page 56).

Steak tartines *with tarragon & paprika butter*

The only slight problem with these little tartines is that they are impossible to eat gracefully. You can make mini versions to serve to your guests as canapés; either way, they are a winner.

MAKES 4

vegetable oil, for frying

1 large red onion, halved and cut into 5mm-thick half moons

1 teaspoon fennel seeds

175g sun-blushed tomatoes in oil, drained

100g Greek yogurt

1–2 teaspoons water, if needed

2 x 200g sirloin steaks

4 large slices of sourdough, toasted

Maldon sea salt flakes and black pepper

FOR THE TARRAGON
& PAPRIKA BUTTER

50g butter, at room temperature

2 garlic cloves, minced

1 heaped teaspoon paprika

½ small packet (about 15g) of tarragon, leaves very finely chopped, plus 4–8 leaves to garnish (optional)

Place a large frying pan over a medium-high heat and drizzle in a little vegetable oil. Add the onion and fennel seeds and stir until well coated in the oil, then cook for 6–8 minutes until slightly charred in places, stirring occasionally. Remove from the pan and transfer to a plate.

Beat the soft butter with the garlic, paprika and tarragon in a small bowl, then season with a generous amount of salt and pepper. Set aside.

Put the sun-blushed tomatoes into a bowl, reserving 4–8 pieces to garnish. Add the yogurt and use a stick blender to blitz until evenly combined and smooth, adding the water if necessary.

Return the frying pan to a high heat. Rub the steaks with a little vegetable oil and season on both sides with a very generous amount of pepper to form a thin pepper crust. Once the pan is very hot, place the steaks in the pan (they should sizzle) and cook for about 2–3 minutes on each side until they are nicely charred. Remove the steaks from the pan and transfer them to a plate, then leave to rest for 10 minutes.

Using a sharp knife, slice the steak very thinly. Place a small saucepan over a medium heat, add the tarragon and paprika butter, and once melted, toss in the steak strips. Remove the pan from the heat and set aside.

Spread the tomato yogurt generously over the toasted bread. Divide the steak between the toasts, top with the onion and reserved tomato and tarragon, if liked. Serve immediately.

Lazy beef & caramelized onion pide

I love Turkish *pide* and Georgian *hachapuri*, but you really need time and patience to make the dough from scratch. This is a quicker, lighter version using puff pastry to satisfy my inner lazy girl, and perfect for sharing – but only if you're in a sharing mood, of course.

MAKES 4

vegetable oil, for frying

2 red onions, halved and very thinly
    sliced into half moons

500g minced beef

1 teaspoon cumin seeds

1 teaspoon ground cinnamon

1 teaspoon chilli flakes

1 teaspoon ground turmeric

2 tablespoons tomato purée

1 red pepper, cored, deseeded and
    finely diced

1 small packet (about 30g) of dill,
    finely chopped

1 small packet (about 30g) of flat leaf
    parsley, finely chopped

50g pine nuts

2 x 320g ready-rolled all-butter
    puff pastry sheets

Maldon sea salt flakes and freshly
    ground black pepper

Preheat the oven to 200°C (180°C fan), Gas Mark 6.

Place a frying pan over a medium heat, drizzle in a little oil and fry the onions for 25–30 minutes until very soft and caramelized, stirring occasionally to prevent browning too much.

Add the minced beef to the pan and break it up as finely as you can to avoid clumps. While it's still uncooked, add the cumin seeds, cinnamon, chilli flakes, turmeric and tomato purée, and mix well into the meat, then continue cooking the meat until it is well browned. Add the red pepper and stir-fry until softened. Season generously with salt and pepper, then remove the pan from the heat and stir through the herbs and pine nuts. Set aside.

Cut each pastry sheet in half lengthways to make 4 long rectangles, then lay these on to baking trays. Divide the meat mixture between the pastry rectangles, leaving a generous border of pastry around the edges. Using your index finger and thumb, make small twists in the pastry edges to form slightly raised crimps. Taper either end of each pastry into a point to form a boat shape. Bake for about 25–30 minutes, or until the pastry is a deep golden brown. Serve immediately.

SIMPLY DELICIOUS WITH...

Carrot, Pistachio & Dill Salad with Lime & Honey Dressing (see page 51).

Lamb, tomato & barley soup

Soups, or *aash* as we call them in Persian, are a staple of the nation. They are far heartier than most other soups and while this isn't a traditional recipe, using barley certainly is. Think of this less as a soup and more as a comforting one-pot meal.

SERVES 8

800g lamb neck fillets, cut in half
    lengthways and cut into 1cm cubes
60g plain flour
75g butter
2 large white onions, finely chopped
4 fat garlic cloves, thinly sliced
4 tablespoons tomato purée
olive oil, for frying
1 tablespoon dried mint
5 large tomatoes, roughly diced
1 litre lamb or vegetable stock

1 litre cold water
finely grated zest and juice of
    1 unwaxed lemon
100g pearl barley
1 small packet (about 30g) of chives,
    finely snipped
Maldon sea salt flakes and freshly
    ground black pepper
crème fraîche or soured cream,
    to serve (optional)

Heat a large saucepan over a medium heat. Meanwhile, dust the pieces of lamb with the flour, shaking off any excess. Add the butter to the pan, and once melted, brown the lamb on all sides.

Add the onions, garlic, tomato purée and a little olive oil to the pan, mix well and fry for a few minutes, then add the dried mint and tomatoes and stir until coated in the onion mixture.

Pour in the stock and cold water and add the lemon zest and juice and a generous amount of salt and pepper. Bring the contents of the pan to a rolling boil, then reduce the heat to low, cover the pan with a lid but leave it slightly ajar and simmer gently for 1 hour, stirring occasionally. Check the liquid level of the soup and top it up a little with water if the broth has reduced too much, as once you add the barley it will absorb some of the liquid.

Replace the pan lid as before and simmer the soup for a further 30 minutes before adding the barley to the pot, stirring well as it goes in. Cook, uncovered, for another 45 minutes or until the barley is cooked, then taste and adjust the seasoning if necessary.

Remove the pan from the heat, stir in the chives just before serving (saving some for a garnish) and dollop a little crème fraîche or soured cream on top with the reserved chives.

Chilled cucumber & pistachio soup

Inspired by the Spanish chilled almond soup *ajo blanco*, I came up with a Persian variation that not only utilizes our most revered nut, but the addition of cucumber dilutes its creaminess a little and makes it the perfect light refreshment all year round. Back in my catering days, I would serve it in shot glasses as an interesting canapé or pre-starter, or middle course. It really is fantastic stuff and even better with some nice crusty bread on the side.

SERVES 4

100g pistachio slivers (or very roughly chopped whole nuts), plus extra to garnish

1 small onion, peeled and quartered

1 large cucumber, peeled and roughly chopped

1 small packet (about 30g) of dill, roughly chopped, reserving 4 sprigs, to garnish

1 small packet (about 30g) of mint, leaves picked

2 garlic cloves, roughly chopped

1 small slice of crusty bread, roughly chopped

1 tablespoon vegan red wine vinegar

200ml cold water

Maldon sea salt flakes and freshly ground black pepper

olive oil, for drizzling

Put the pistachios, onion, cucumber, herbs, garlic, bread and vinegar into a blender and blitz until smooth.

Season to taste with salt and pepper, then add the cold water and briefly whizz to combine and thin the purée to a soup consistency. Serve immediately, drizzled with olive oil. Scatter with extra pistachio slivers and add a dill sprig to garnish.

SIMPLY DELICIOUS WITH...

Strawberry, Soft Goats' Cheese & Pistachio Salad (see page 179) or Harissa Kofta Lettuce Cups with Preserved Lemon Yogurt (see page 123).

Tomato & peanut salad
with tamarind, ginger & honey dressing

I find myself turning to tamarind as a flavour base more and more these days. It offers the acidity that both lemons and vinegar do, but is still not remotely as overpowering as either of those ingredients. In fact, pair it with something sweet such as honey, and you still get the acidity but in a wonderfully gentle and well-rounded capacity. Here, it makes the perfect dressing for this simple salad of tomatoes, and the ginger adds another flavour dimension that makes it impossible not to keep eating this salad until it's all gone.

SERVES 4—6

1 small red onion, finely chopped

200g baby tomatoes, halved

2 handfuls of salted peanuts

1 small packet (about 30g) of fresh
    coriander, roughly chopped

FOR THE DRESSING

7cm piece of fresh root ginger, peeled
    and finely grated

2 tablespoons olive oil

1 heaped tablespoon unsweetened
    tamarind paste

1 tablespoon light soy sauce

1 tablespoon clear honey

small amount of Maldon sea salt flakes

freshly ground black pepper

Mix all the dressing ingredients together in a small bowl. Add the onion and leave to soak for about 20 minutes to soften.

Add the tomatoes, peanuts and coriander to a bowl. Pour over the onion and dressing and mix together well. Serve the salad at room temperature.

SIMPLY DELICIOUS WITH...

Chorizo, Goats' Cheese & Cumin Borek (see page 148) or Goats' Cheese, Vegetable & Za'atar Filo Tart (see page 207).

TIP
Substitute agave syrup or caster sugar for the honey to make this recipe suitable for vegans.

Sweetcorn, black bean & avocado salad

Sweetcorn reminds me of my childhood, when I usually ate it straight from the can, but as an adult I prefer to cook whole sweetcorn cobs and enjoy the rich, intense sweetness of the kernels. A good corn salad can be the perfect pairing with so many ingredients, but my travels to Thailand have inspired the addition of kaffir lime leaves for a flavour like no other. This is a spicy salad, which, of course, you can tame by using less chilli, but I've served this to people who aren't chilli lovers and they enjoyed it so much that I decided to share the recipe here with you.

SERVES 10—12

6 sweetcorn cobs

2 avocados, peeled, stoned and diced

400g can black beans, drained and rinsed

4 kaffir lime leaves, very finely chopped

4 spring onions, thinly sliced

1 small red pepper, cored, deseeded and finely diced

1 small green pepper, cored, deseeded and finely diced

2 long red chillies, deseeded and finely chopped

1 small packet (about 30g) of fresh coriander, finely chopped

2 heaped tablespoons mayonnaise

drizzle of olive oil

Maldon sea salt flakes and freshly ground black pepper

Cook the sweetcorn cobs in a saucepan of boiling water for about 10 minutes until tender. Drain and rinse under cold running water until cool, then drain again.

Hold each cob in turn upright on a chopping board and, using a sharp knife, cut from the top to the bottom to slice off the kernels in strips.

Put the sweetcorn kernels into a bowl with all the remaining ingredients and mix together well. Season to taste with salt and pepper and serve.

SIMPLY DELICIOUS WITH...

Harissa & Lime Chicken Wings (see page 116) or Spiced Pork Wraps with Green Apple Salsa (see page 167).

TIP

This is a large salad, so halve the ingredients to make a smaller batch.

Chargrilled aubergines
with red pepper, chilli & walnut sauce

I often say that aubergines are the meat of the Middle East. Here I pair them with a romesco-inspired sauce, which seasons the aubergine beautifully. Leftovers, as standard, should be piled into some crusty bread with feta cheese – this is my best advice to you and you may just thank me for it.

SERVES 6–8

2 large or 3 small aubergines, cut into
   1cm-thick discs
garlic oil, for brushing
generous handful of green olives,
   pitted
1 small packet (about 30g) of flat leaf
   parsley, roughly chopped
Maldon sea salt flakes and freshly
   ground black pepper

FOR THE SAUCE
1 red pepper, cored, deseeded and
   roughly chopped
1 long red chilli, roughly chopped
50g walnut pieces, plus extra to
   garnish (optional)
1 fat garlic clove, peeled
1 tablespoon red wine vinegar
olive oil

Put all the ingredients for the sauce into a blender with 3 tablespoons of olive oil and blitz until smooth. Season to taste with salt and pepper and set aside.

Heat a nonstick griddle pan over a medium-high heat. Using a pastry brush, brush one side of the aubergine slices with just enough garlic oil to coat the surface. Once the griddle pan is hot, in batches add the aubergine slices, oiled side down, and chargrill for about 6–8 minutes, then brush the top sides with garlic oil before you turn them over and cook for a further 6–8 minutes until nicely charred and cooked through. Remove from the pan and leave to cool. Repeat with the remaining aubergine slices.

Arrange the aubergine slices on a large platter and season them with salt and pepper. Pour the sauce liberally over the aubergines. Top with the olives and parsley, scatter over some extra walnuts to garnish, if liked, and drizzle with a little olive oil before serving.

SIMPLY DELICIOUS WITH...

Marinated Steak with Labneh, Pul Biber Butter & Crispy Onions (see page 188) or Lamb, Cumin, Coriander & Chilli Kebabs (see page 118).

Watermelon, black olive & feta
with cayenne, honey & lime dressing

Feta and watermelon are a typical Eastern pairing, and when I was looking to come up with a recipe using them, I spotted frozen feta on the Instagram of James Cochran, a chef friend of mine, so I borrowed this little trick from him. Freezing the feta enables you to grate it, which means the flavour you get is a rather more subtle saltiness than you would achieve if using chunks of feta. The dressing is really what brings this dish together; sweet and citrusy, it makes it such a great salad for the summer.

SERVES 4—6

about 1kg watermelon, quartered, deseeded and very thinly sliced (like carpaccio)

finely grated zest of 1 fat unwaxed lime

15g chervil (see Tip), leaves roughly chopped

generous handful of Greek basil leaves

2 handfuls of pitted Kalamata olives

100g vegetarian feta cheese, frozen

handful of pistachio slivers (or very roughly chopped whole nuts)

freshly ground black pepper

FOR THE DRESSING

2 tablespoons clear honey

½ teaspoon cayenne pepper

2 tablespoons olive oil

juice of the lime zested above

generous amount of Maldon sea salt flakes

Arrange the watermelon slices on a large platter, season well with pepper and scatter the lime zest over.

Mix the dressing ingredients together in a jug or small bowl and drizzle all over the watermelon, then scatter over the fresh herbs and olives. Remove the frozen feta from the freezer and finely grate over the watermelon, then sprinkle with the pistachios and serve immediately.

SIMPLY DELICIOUS WITH...

Harissa Chicken Noodle Lettuce Cups (see page 115) or Harissa & Lime Chicken Wings (see page 116).

TIP

If you can't find fresh chervil, use fresh mint leaves instead.

Ghayour house chicken kari

Admittedly, this isn't exactly a Persian classic, but every time I make this I am asked for the recipe, so here it is! I hope, like me, you find it to be a very useful, straightforward curry base – you can substitute the chicken with prawns, or use vegetables such as cauliflower, squash, courgettes or root vegetables to make a vegetarian or vegan alternative.

SERVES 4—6

4 tablespoons vegetable oil

1 teaspoon black mustard seeds

1 teaspoon fenugreek seeds

1 teaspoon cumin seeds

1 teaspoon coriander seeds

1 cassia bark stick (not a cinnamon stick, as they are too strong)

3 cardamom pods, crushed

1 large onion, very finely chopped

7.5cm piece of fresh root ginger, peeled and grated or very finely chopped

4 fat garlic cloves, bashed and thinly sliced

1–2 small green 'rocket' chillies or 1–2 large long red chillies to taste, stalks intact and split

8 large bone-in, skinless chicken thighs

2 teaspoons ground turmeric

4 large tomatoes, roughly diced

400g can chopped tomatoes

Maldon sea salt flakes and freshly ground black pepper

flatbreads or steamed rice, to serve

Place a large saucepan over a medium-high heat and pour in the vegetable oil. Add the mustard, fenugreek, cumin and coriander seeds, the cassia bark and cardamom pods and fry, shaking the pan, until the mustard seeds begin to pop. Stir in the onion and fry for a few minutes until it begins to brown and caramelize but without burning.

Add the ginger, garlic and chillies to the pan and briefly stir-fry for a minute or so, then add the chicken thighs, turmeric and a generous amount of salt and pepper and stir until the chicken is well coated in the onion and spice mixture. Add the fresh tomatoes followed by the canned tomatoes, then pour over just enough cold water to cover the chicken. Reduce the heat and gently simmer for 2 hours, stirring occasionally to prevent it sticking or catching and topping up the liquid level with a little cold water if necessary.

Remove the cassia bark and cardamom pods, then check and adjust the seasoning before serving with flatbreads or steamed rice.

SIMPLY DELICIOUS WITH... Adas Polow (see page 101).

Sticky harissa, sesame & pistachio chicken

This recipe embodies all the qualities I like in a chicken dish – sticky, savoury, spicy, crunchy and utterly delicious. It reminds me of Cantonese sticky chicken dishes, but with a little more oomph and, more importantly, it can be easily recreated at home.

SERVES 3—4

500g boneless, skinless chicken
   breasts
vegetable oil, for frying
1 teaspoon ground cinnamon
1 teaspoon garlic granules
3 tablespoons clear honey

2 tablespoons rose harissa
25g sesame seeds, toasted
50g pistachio nuts, roughly chopped
Maldon sea salt flakes and freshly
   ground black pepper

Lay the chicken breasts flat on a chopping board and roughly chop into fillets.

Heat a large frying pan over a high heat and drizzle in a little vegetable oil. Once hot, add the chicken strips and quickly toss in the oil. Sear the chicken on the outside until opaque all over but not cooked through.

Add the cinnamon and garlic granules and quickly toss the chicken in them, then add the honey and harissa and stir until the chicken is well coated. Season with a generous amount of salt and pepper. Leave the chicken to cook for about 1 minute until cooked through, then stir to coat in the sauce.

Once the sauce is bubbling and reduced to an almost caramel-like consistency, remove the pan from the heat, stir and sprinkle with the toasted sesame seeds and the pistachios before serving.

SIMPLY DELICIOUS WITH...

Carrot, Pistachio & Dill Salad with Lime & Honey Dressing (see page 51) or Tomato & Peanut Salad with Tamarind, Ginger & Honey Dressing (see page 137).

TIP

You can also use mini chicken fillets for this recipe.

Chorizo, goats' cheese & cumin borek

Although not a traditional borek filling, this wonderful combination of smoky, spiced chorizo and cumin-spiked, creamy goats' cheese is a winner. Chorizo really is such a fantastic ingredient and its capability to deliver bags of flavour to anything it comes into contact with always makes it a crowd-pleaser and a refrigerator staple in my household.

SERVES 4—6

2 x 200g cured (not cooking) chorizo sausages, skinned and cut into chunks

2 teaspoons cumin seeds, toasted

350g rindless soft goats' cheese

vegetable oil, for oiling

6 sheets of filo pastry (each about 48 x 25cm)

1 tablespoon milk or water

beaten egg, to glaze

1 teaspoon nigella seeds

Preheat the oven to 200°C (180°C fan), Gas Mark 6.

Put the chunks of chorizo into a food processor and process until they are minced as finely as possible. Transfer to a mixing bowl, add the cumin seeds and goats' cheese and mix together until evenly combined.

Brush the base of a 24cm round ovenproof dish or cake tin with a little vegetable oil. Lay a pastry sheet lengthways in the dish or tin with the ends overhanging the sides, then lay another pastry sheet widthways in the same way. Divide the chorizo filling in half. Add one half to the filo base and smooth it right to the edges to cover the base evenly. Fold another pastry sheet in half to create a double thickness and lay it over the filling, then repeat with a second pastry sheet to form a thick pastry layer. Brush the pastry with the milk or water, then top with the remaining filling, pushing and patting it into place to evenly coat the pastry layer. Fold the overhanging pastry into the centre, then gently crumple up the remaining 2 pastry sheets and arrange them on top.

Brush all the exposed pastry and edges with beaten egg and sprinkle over the nigella seeds. Bake for 25–30 minutes until deep golden brown. Serve immediately.

SIMPLY DELICIOUS WITH...
Pear, Chickpea & Green Leaf Salad with Maple Harissa Dressing (see page 172).

Silk Road-style lamb & cumin pasta

I know this sounds like a weird combination to be thrown over pasta and I know it may seem like it's cumin-heavy (which it is), but it really works, and I have won over quite a few sceptics with this recipe, mostly because it's actually, and perhaps for some surprisingly, very delicious and satisfying. Try it – it's one of my favourite recipes in this book and I knew instantly that I had to share it with you.

SERVES 4

500g lamb leg steaks or other
    lamb steaks

1 tablespoon garlic granules

2 tablespoons cumin seeds, toasted
    and ground (see Tip on page 15)

1 tablespoon chilli flakes

1 teaspoon ground cinnamon

1 teaspoon ground coriander

3 tablespoons olive oil

1 teaspoon toasted sesame oil

4 tablespoons light soy sauce, or more
    to taste

1 teaspoon rice vinegar

250g tagliatelle

50g butter

Maldon sea salt flakes and freshly
    ground black pepper

Place the lamb steaks between 2 layers of clingfilm and bash the meat with a meat tenderizer or the flat side of a rolling pin to flatten and tenderize the meat. Discard the clingfilm and thinly slice the lamb into strips about 5mm thick. Place the lamb strips in a non-reactive bowl, add the garlic granules, spices, oils, soy sauce, vinegar and a generous amount of salt and pepper and mix together well. Cover the bowl with clingfilm and leave to marinate at room temperature for at least 1 hour.

Cook the tagliatelle in a large saucepan of salted boiling water according to the packet instructions, then drain the pasta, reserving the cooking water.

Meanwhile, heat a wok or large frying pan over a high heat. Once hot, add the lamb along with the marinade and cook for a few minutes until seared all over, but avoid stirring constantly. Remove the pan from the heat to ensure the meat stays slightly rare and tender. Add the butter and check and adjust the seasoning, adding more salt, pepper or soy sauce to taste. Add the cooked pasta together with 2–3 ladles of the reserved pasta water and mix well with tongs, adding more of the cooking water to the pasta to loosen, if liked. Serve immediately, no accompaniment needed.

Fragrant fish cakes
with preserved lemon mayonnaise

Many Brits avoid dill with white fish (especially if you grew up in 1980s England eating vacuum-packed white fish in dill sauce), but it still remains one of my favourite pairings. The preserved lemon mayo provides a really decent hit of salty citrus that works incredibly well with the fish cakes.

MAKES 6–8

FOR THE FISH CAKES
vegetable oil, for frying
300g skinless chunky white fish fillet,
    such as cod, hake or haddock, diced
400g mashed potatoes
1 small packet (about 30g) of dill,
    finely chopped
1 small packet (about 30g) of fresh
    coriander, finely chopped
2 tablespoons English mustard
    powder
4 tablespoons plain flour

1 teaspoon chilli flakes
1 teaspoon ground ginger
1 teaspoon garlic granules
1 egg
Maldon sea salt flakes and freshly ground
    black pepper

FOR THE PRESERVED LEMON
MAYONNAISE
3 small preserved lemons, deseeded and
    finely chopped
4 heaped tablespoons mayonnaise

Place a frying pan over a gentle heat, drizzle in a tiny amount of oil and add the fish. Cook for 6–8 minutes until just opaque. Transfer the fish to a sieve, break into flakes and leave to drain.

Preheat your oven to its highest setting.

Put the fish with all the remaining fish cake ingredients into a mixing bowl and season well with salt and pepper. Using your hands, work the ingredients together really well, pummelling the mixture for several minutes into a smooth, even paste – the more you work the mixture, the better it will bind together. Shape into 6–8 patties. Place the patties on a baking tray and bake for 12 minutes until just starting to brown. Remove from the oven and finish cooking the fish cakes in a hot frying pan with a drizzle of oil for 4–6 minutes on each side, or until nicely browned.

Mix the preserved lemons with the mayonnaise in a small bowl, season with pepper and serve with the hot fish cakes.

SIMPLY DELICIOUS WITH…
Green Bean Salad with Tahini, Preserved Lemon & Pine Nuts (see page 47).

Fish, okra & tamarind stew

I dedicate this recipe to my dear friend Bryan Koh, who I first met in Singapore and who took me to some of the best places in town for local cuisine, including fish head curry. Sadly, it isn't something we get to eat very often back home in England, so I came up with a version that we make at home and enjoy while thinking of Bryan.

SERVES 4—6

100g fresh root ginger, peeled

25g fresh turmeric, unpeeled and scrubbed

1 onion, cut into rough chunks

4 garlic cloves, peeled

vegetable oil, for frying

3 cardamom pods, bashed

1 teaspoon cumin seeds

1 teaspoon fennel seeds

1 teaspoon chilli flakes

1 teaspoon ground coriander

1 teaspoon ground turmeric

300g fresh okra (or use frozen whole okra, defrosted)

3 tomatoes, roughly diced

1 tablespoon unsweetened tamarind paste

500g skinless chunky white fish fillet, such as cod, hake or haddock, cut into 4cm chunks

Maldon sea salt flakes and generous amount of freshly ground black pepper

Put the ginger, fresh turmeric, onion and garlic into a mini food processor and blitz to as fine a paste as you can achieve.

Place a saucepan over a medium heat, drizzle in a little vegetable oil and add the paste. Cook for 8–10 minutes until all the moisture has evaporated and the paste has mixed with the oil, ensuring it doesn't catch.

Add the dry spices and salt and pepper and stir. Add the okra and stir to coat it in the mixture, then stir in the tomatoes and tamarind paste. Pour in just enough water to cover the ingredients, cover the pan with a lid and leave to simmer over a gentle heat for 30 minutes until the sauce thickens, stirring occasionally to prevent sticking. If you have a lot of liquid left in the pan, remove the lid and cook over a slightly higher heat for a few minutes until it has reduced.

Place the fish chunks on top of the stew, cover the pan with the lid and cook for 5 minutes. Remove the lid, spoon the okra and sauce over the fish and cook for a further 5 minutes. Serve with rice.

SIMPLY DELICIOUS WITH... Adas Polow (see page 101).

Seafood, coconut & ginger spiced rice

The Spanish have the right idea with their famous pan-baked rice dish of paella, and while this isn't a paella, it's put together in a similar manner, albeit using very different flavours. I am a big lover of rice and I think it makes a fantastic partner for seafood. This spiced coconut and ginger rice is rich, comforting and has a depth of flavour that makes it incredibly delicious. The best part? You can take it straight from the hob to the table; one-pot cooking at its finest.

SERVES 4—6

2 tablespoons olive oil

1 onion, finely chopped

7.5cm piece of fresh root ginger, peeled and sliced into thin matchsticks

200g Spanish paella rice

1 heaped teaspoon curry powder

1 teaspoon ground turmeric

200ml coconut milk

200ml cold water

200g frozen squid tubes, defrosted and each cut into 3–4 rings

200g baby plum tomatoes, halved

6 large raw prawns in their shells

Maldon sea salt flakes and freshly ground black pepper

Place a wide pan, ideally nonstick, over a medium heat and pour in the olive oil. Add the onion and cook for a few minutes until it begins to turn translucent. Add the ginger, stirring to ensure it doesn't burn. Continue cooking gently until both the onion and ginger are softened, without browning.

Add the rice and stir until well coated with the onion and ginger, then stir in the curry powder, turmeric and a generous amount of salt and pepper.

Pour in the coconut milk, cold water, squid and tomatoes and mix well. Lay the prawns on top, reduce the heat slightly and cook gently for about 20 minutes. Cover the pan with a lid and cook for a further 10 minutes until the prawns turn pink, then remove the lid and cook for a final 10 minutes until the rice is cooked through. Serve immediately.

SIMPLY DELICIOUS WITH...

Carrot, Pistachio & Dill Salad with Lime & Honey Dressing (see page 51) or Fennel Salad with Spinach, Cashew & Coriander Seed Dressing (see page 53).

Something special

Crispy cod wraps *with salsa & harissa lime mayo*

I sometimes find that fish can be a bit of a hard sell to some folk, but this is the perfect recipe for converting fussy eaters.

MAKES 6

2 eggs

100g plain flour

1 tablespoon garlic granules

1 tablespoon English mustard powder

2 teaspoons paprika

1 teaspoon cayenne pepper

1 teaspoon ground turmeric

vegetable oil, for frying

500g cod loins, cut into 2.5cm chunks

6 mini tortilla wraps

Maldon sea salt flakes and black pepper

FOR THE SALSA

2 tomatoes, very finely diced

½ onion, very finely diced

½ small packet (about 15g) dill, chopped

drizzle of olive oil

1 teaspoon caster sugar

FOR THE HARISSA LIME MAYO

3 tablespoons mayonnaise

1 tablespoon rose harissa

finely grated zest of 1 lime and juice of ½

Maldon sea salt flakes

First make the salsa: combine the tomatoes, onion and dill in a bowl, add the olive oil and sugar and season well with salt and pepper, then mix together and set aside.

Mix the mayonnaise ingredients together in a small bowl and set aside.

Crack the eggs into a small shallow bowl, season with a little salt and pepper and beat together. Put the flour, garlic granules, mustard powder and spices into a separate small shallow bowl, season very generously with salt and generously with pepper and mix until well combined.

Pour enough vegetable oil into a deep frying pan to fill to a depth of 2cm. Heat the oil over a medium-high heat and bring to frying temperature. Line a plate with kitchen paper.

Coat each piece of fish evenly in the flour mixture, then dip into the beaten egg to coat, and finally dip once more in the flour mixture, ensuring each piece is well coated. When the oil is ready (dip a piece of fish into the oil: if it sizzles immediately the oil is hot enough; if it bubbles ferociously the oil is too hot so reduce the heat before you begin cooking), fry the fish in batches for about 2–3 minutes, or until the batter is crispy and deep golden brown. Transfer to the paper-lined plate to drain. Serve in wraps with the mayo and top with a little of the salsa.

SIMPLY DELICIOUS WITH...

Baked Sweet Potato, Za'atar & Garlic Chips (see page 34).

Sticky peach & halloumi skewers

I love halloumi so much that I am always trying to come up with quick and easy ways to make it shine. It's a refrigerator staple in my house, and when I'm exhausted I tend to turn to halloumi, so I have learned to be a bit creative with it. This recipe, like so many of my recipes, was born out of convenience. A simple store-cupboard and spice-rack raid, and suddenly the humble halloumi is transformed into something utterly indulgent. This also happens to make for great sharing or finger food.

MAKES 12

2 x 250g blocks of halloumi cheese

4 heaped tablespoons apricot or
    peach jam

1 teaspoon chilli flakes

1 heaped teaspoon dried wild thyme

1 teaspoon garlic granules

olive oil, for frying

2 tablespoons cold water

3 large ripe peaches (or nectarines),
    stoned and cut into 8 wedges

freshly ground black pepper

Cut each block of halloumi in half lengthways, then cut each half into 3 equal-sized cubes to make 12 cubes in total.

Put the jam, chilli flakes, thyme, garlic granules and a generous amount of pepper into a small bowl and mix together until evenly combined.

Place a frying pan over a medium heat and brush the pan with a little olive oil to just lightly coat the base. Add the halloumi cubes and fry for about 1 minute on each side until nicely browned all over, then remove from the pan and set aside. Rinse or wipe out the pan with kitchen paper.

Add the jam mixture to the pan along with the measured cold water, stir and heat until it reaches a glaze consistency. Return the halloumi to the pan and turn to coat with the glaze, then remove the pan from the heat.

Take 12 small skewers and thread each with a wedge of peach (or nectarine), then a cube of halloumi followed by another wedge of peach to finish. Serve immediately.

SIMPLY DELICIOUS WITH...

Crispy Prawns with a Mango & Tomato Dip (see page 164) or Harissa Chicken Noodle Lettuce Cups (see page 115).

Crispy prawns *with a mango & tomato dip*

Salt and pepper squid has always been a favourite of mine, but I'd never thought of giving prawns the same treatment until I first saw them on a restaurant menu. I've since experimented with different spice coatings on all kinds of fish and seafood, and this is a lovely combination that works really well with the accompanying dip.

SERVES 2

4 tablespoons cornflour
1 heaped teaspoon ground turmeric
1 heaped teaspoon garlic granules
1 heaped teaspoon curry powder
1 teaspoon paprika
16 large raw prawns, peeled but tails left on
vegetable oil, for frying
generous amount of Maldon sea salt flakes
   and freshly ground black pepper

FOR THE MANGO & TOMATO DIP

1 ripe tomato
handful of very ripe mango flesh
3cm piece of fresh root ginger, peeled
   and roughly chopped
2 tablespoons tomato ketchup
1 tablespoon Tabasco sauce
1 tablespoon caster sugar
Maldon sea salt flakes and freshly ground
   black pepper

Put all the ingredients for the dip into a blender and blitz until smooth. Transfer to a bowl.

Combine the dry ingredients, including the salt and pepper. Add the prawns and coat well.

Pour enough vegetable oil into a large, deep frying pan or saucepan to fill to a depth of about 2.5cm. Heat the oil over a medium-high heat and bring to frying temperature (carefully dip one of the prawns in the oil: if it sizzles immediately, the oil is ready). Line a plate with a double layer of kitchen paper.

Fry the prawns in batches for a few minutes (1 minute for small prawns, and up to 3 minutes for large prawns as pictured), or until crisp, golden and cooked through. Remove the crispy prawns with a slotted spoon and transfer to the paper-lined plate to drain. Serve immediately with the dip.

SIMPLY DELICIOUS WITH…

Spring Onion Salad with Sesame & Pul Biber (see page 41) or Sweetcorn, Black Bean & Avocado Salad (see page 139).

TIP
If your mango isn't ripe, try adding some mango chutney or apricot jam to bolster the sweetness of the dip.

Spiced pork wraps
with green apple salsa

Pork and apple is a classic combination, and the sweet yet tangy apple certainly does so much to complement the meat, but pack in some spices and you take it to a whole other level. Think of these as a kind of taco, one of my favourite things to eat – messy, gratifying and utterly delicious. I particularly enjoy food that can be eaten using your hands and where the finished components can be plated up and served to guests so that you can all pile in and it becomes a shared, convivial meal together.

SERVES 4—6

800g boneless pork shoulder,
    cut into 2.5cm cubes
vegetable oil
8–12 mini tortilla wraps
    (or pitta breads or flatbreads)
¼ head of iceberg lettuce,
    very finely shredded
Maldon sea salt flakes and
    freshly ground black pepper

FOR THE MARINADE

4–5 tablespoons hot chilli sauce,
    such as Tabasco or Sriracha, to taste
3 tablespoons caster sugar
2 tablespoons rice vinegar
1 teaspoon smoked paprika
1 teaspoon ground coriander
1 teaspoon ground cumin
1 teaspoon ground cinnamon

FOR THE SALSA

2 green apples, cored and very finely
    diced
1 small packet (about 30g) of fresh
    coriander, very finely chopped
1 small red onion, very finely chopped
½ teaspoon nigella seeds
1 tablespoon clear honey
1 tablespoon olive oil

TO SERVE

Greek yogurt
sweet chilli sauce

CONTINUED OVERLEAF

Put all the ingredients for the marinade into a plastic food container with a generous amount of salt and pepper and mix well. Add the pork and use your hands to coat it in the marinade, then massage the meat a little to allow the marinade to work its way into the pork. Seal the container with the lid and leave to marinate in the refrigerator for a few hours, or overnight.

Preheat the oven to 180°C (160°C fan), Gas Mark 4.

Mix all the salsa ingredients together in a small bowl, season to taste with salt and pepper and set aside.

Place a frying pan over a high heat and add a drizzle of vegetable oil. Once hot, use tongs to add a batch of the marinated pieces of pork to the pan, without overcrowding, leaving as much of the marinade behind as you can (otherwise it will burn and cause the meat to stew instead of fry). Cook for 1–2 minutes until you have a nice dark crust on the underside, then turn the meat over and cook on the other side for 1–2 minutes until cooked through. Remove from the pan and cook the remaining meat in the same way.

Meanwhile, wrap your tortillas or chosen breads in foil and warm through in the oven.

Place a little shredded lettuce on to each wrap, add the pork and some salsa, then top with a little dollop of Greek yogurt and a drizzle of sweet chilli sauce. Serve immediately.

SIMPLY DELICIOUS WITH...

Spring Onion Salad with Sesame & Pul Biber (see page 41) and Baked Sweet Potato, Za'atar & Garlic Chips (see page 34).

Chicken & apricot pastries

Growing up in a nation that makes savoury pies and pastries like no other means constantly craving and coming up with new and interesting fillings to wrap in a variety of different pastries to keep myself satisfied. The first time I made these was when I had leftover roast chicken and builders had set up scaffolding outside my apartment. Let's just say it was the perfect welcoming gesture that kept them friendly and kind for the duration of our relationship.

MAKES 8

vegetable oil

1 large onion, finely chopped

300g boneless, skinless chicken thighs

2 teaspoons curry powder

1 teaspoon ground turmeric

1 teaspoon ground cinnamon

100g ready-to-eat dried apricots, very thinly sliced

1 tablespoon apricot jam

juice of ½ lemon

1 small packet (about 30g) of flat leaf parsley, finely chopped

2 x 320g ready-rolled all-butter puff pastry sheets

1 egg, beaten

1 teaspoon nigella seeds

Maldon sea salt flakes and freshly ground black pepper

Place a large saucepan over a medium heat and pour in enough vegetable oil to coat the base of the pan. Add the onion and cook for a few minutes until softened and translucent, without browning.

Add the chicken, spices and salt and pepper and stir to coat the chicken well. Pour in enough boiling water to cover the ingredients, then simmer over a gentle heat for 1 hour until the chicken is cooked through and tender. Remove from the heat and leave to cool.

Remove the chicken from the pan and finely chop, then put into a bowl. Add the apricots, jam and lemon juice, along with the remaining sauce from the pan and the parsley, then using your hands, mix well to ensure the chicken is thoroughly coated.

CONTINUED OVERLEAF

Preheat the oven to 220°C (200°C fan), Gas Mark 7. Line a large baking tray with baking paper.

Cut each pastry sheet into 4 squares. Divide the chicken mixture into 8 and form into sausage shapes. Lay a sausage shape diagonally on each pastry square, then fold over the corners of each pastry square and pinch together to seal. Place smooth side up on the prepared baking tray, brush with the beaten egg and sprinkle with the nigella seeds. Bake for 20–22 minutes until a deep golden colour. Leave to cool slightly before serving.

SIMPLY DELICIOUS WITH...

Green-yogurt-dressed Baby Gem Lettuce with Burnt Hazelnuts (see page 44) and Carrot, Pistachio & Dill Salad with Lime & Honey Dressing (see page 51).

Pear, chickpea & green leaf salad
with maple harissa dressing

I love using fresh fruit in salads, from apples and oranges to luscious ripe berries, but the intense sweetness of pears means they can stand up to much bolder flavours like blue cheese and, most valuable to me, chilli and spice. This is a great combination and the addition of chickpeas makes it ever so much more than a salad. The maple syrup and harissa work like magic to dress the ingredients, and I promise you, this is a wonderful addition to any table.

SERVES 4—6

50g rocket leaves

50g watercress

2 pears, halved, cored and
    thinly sliced

400g can chickpeas, drained
    and rinsed

handful of sunflower seeds, to garnish

FOR THE DRESSING

1 generous tablespoon maple syrup

1 tablespoon olive oil

juice of ½ lemon

1 teaspoon rose harissa

generous amount of Maldon sea salt flakes
    and freshly ground black pepper

Arrange the salad leaves, pear slices and chickpeas in a large shallow bowl or on a platter.

Mix all the dressing ingredients together in a jug or small bowl, then pour over the salad. Sprinkle with the sunflower seeds to garnish and serve immediately.

SIMPLY DELICIOUS WITH…

Chorizo, Goats' Cheese & Cumin Borek (see page 148) or Goats' Cheese, Vegetable & Za'atar Filo Tart (see page 207).

Cauliflower & asparagus black rice salad

Cauliflower is an absolutely cracking addition to a salad, and here I've paired it with my other love, rice – in particular, beautiful dark black rice. Any leftovers make the most wonderful packed lunch the next day – if there are any leftovers, of course.

SERVES 6—8

200g black Venus rice

400ml water

1 cauliflower, cut into florets

250g asparagus tips

50g fresh coriander, roughly chopped

25g dill, roughly chopped, plus extra
    to garnish

25g flat leaf parsley, roughly chopped

6 tablespoons olive oil

200g natural yogurt

squeeze of lemon juice

2–3 preserved lemons, to taste

½ teaspoon pul biber chilli flakes

Maldon sea salt flakes and freshly
    ground black pepper

Put the rice and the water in a saucepan and bring to the boil, then cover the pan, reduce the heat and simmer for 35–45 minutes, or according to the packet instructions, until tender.

Meanwhile, cook the cauliflower florets in a separate pan of boiling water for 10 minutes, then drain and rinse under cold running water. Set aside. Blanch the asparagus tips in another pan of boiling water for 3 minutes, then plunge into cold water to cool and leave to drain.

Put the coriander, dill and parsley into a mini food processor with 4 tablespoons of the olive oil and 6 tablespoons of cold water and blitz until smooth. Season well with salt and pepper, then stir into the yogurt in a bowl and add the lemon juice. Set aside.

Place a nonstick griddle pan over a high heat. Drizzle over and rub the asparagus with the remaining 2 tablespoons of olive oil. Once the griddle pan is hot, chargrill the asparagus for 2 minutes on each side, then set aside.

Arrange the rice on a platter, top with the cauliflower and asparagus and dollop with the yogurt mixture. Thinly slice the preserved lemons and arrange on top, then sprinkle over the pul biber and garnish with dill before serving.

SIMPLY DELICIOUS WITH...
Turmeric Chicken Kebabs (see page 24) and Yogurt & Spice Roasted Salmon (see page 62).

Roasted parsnips
with tahini yogurt sauce, herb oil & pomegranate seeds

I've always thought of parsnips as one of my favourite root vegetables and I can't understand why they seem to be only eaten at Christmas. My friend Mathew hates parsnips, and while I did win him over with the harissa and honey-roasted parsnips in my book *Bazaar*, I am hoping this will seal the deal and put parsnips firmly on the menu for him.

SERVES 4—6

1kg parsnips, peeled and halved
    lengthways
garlic oil, for drizzling
2 sprigs of tarragon, leaves picked
4 sprigs of flat leaf parsley
3–4 tablespoons olive oil
2 squeezes of lemon juice

1 tablespoon tahini
1–2 tablespoons warm water
4 tablespoons Greek yogurt
75g pomegranate seeds
Maldon sea salt flakes and freshly ground
    black pepper

Preheat the oven to 200°C (180°C fan), Gas Mark 6.

Place the parsnips on a large baking tray, drizzle with garlic oil and season with a generous amount of salt and pepper, then use your hands to mix until the parsnips are well coated in the oil and seasoning. Spread the parsnips out on the baking tray and roast for about 30–35 minutes (depending on their size and thickness) until nicely browned and tender.

Meanwhile, put the tarragon and parsley into a blender with the olive oil, a squeeze of the lemon juice and salt and pepper and blitz until you have a smooth herb oil. Set aside.

To make the sauce, mix together the tahini, the remaining squeeze of lemon juice and 1 tablespoon of warm water (not cold water, otherwise the tahini will seize) in a small bowl, then beat in the yogurt and season to taste with salt. Add another tablespoon of warm water if you prefer a thinner consistency.

Once the parsnips are done, arrange them on a platter and drizzle the tahini yogurt sauce over, then drizzle with the herb oil. Finally, sprinkle over the pomegranate seeds before serving.

SIMPLY DELICIOUS WITH...

Spice-rubbed Spatchcocked Poussin (see page 55) or Pot-roasted Brisket with Harissa & Spices (see page 59).

Strawberry, soft goats' cheese & pistachio salad

In the early 1990s I once made a salad using strawberries to impress my friends. I must admit it went down like a lead balloon, being perhaps too avant garde at the time. This recipe, however, is one I created with confidence and have served several times when strawberries are in season and bursting with sweetness – they dress the salad with their natural juices. The soft, mild goats' cheese works so well with the strawberries, and pistachios add not only a vibrant colour, but also a wonderful crunch. A perfect summer salad to go with any meal.

SERVES 4–6

400g strawberries

5 basil leaves

5 large mint leaves

150g soft, mild rindless goats' cheese, torn into small chunks

50g pistachio nuts, roughly chopped

½ teaspoon sumac

½ teaspoon pul biber chilli flakes

freshly ground black pepper

FOR THE DRESSING

2 tablespoons olive oil

juice of ½ lemon

1 generous tablespoon clear honey

Hull the strawberries and then cut them into quarters. Stack the basil leaves one on top of the other, roll them up together and then finely slice the roll widthways to cut the basil into thin ribbons. Repeat with the mint leaves.

Arrange the strawberries on a platter and scatter over the goats' cheese and herbs. Add the pistachios and sprinkle with the sumac and pul biber.

Mix the dressing ingredients together in a jug or small bowl. Season the salad with plenty of pepper, then drizzle the dressing over and serve.

SIMPLY DELICIOUS WITH...

Green Chicken (see page 23) or Harissa Kofta Lettuce Cups with Preserved Lemon Yogurt (see page 123).

TIP

Try substituting feta for the goats' cheese.

Spiced chicory & roasted pepper salad *with oranges & anchovies*

Also known as Rob's Birthday Salad as I created this for the special birthday of a good friend of mine. I've never met anyone who was so into anchovies – I am a relatively new convert. This salad embodies all the flavours and components that I feel complement the saltiness of the anchovies – bitter, sweet, sharp and nutty.

SERVES 4—6

300g baby peppers, halved, cored and
   deseeded
4 oranges
2 large heads of chicory, leaves separated
50g anchovy fillets
generous handful of pine nuts
Maldon sea salt flakes and black pepper

FOR THE DRESSING

3 tablespoons olive oil, plus extra
   for drizzling
2 tablespoons red wine vinegar
1 generous tablespoon clear honey
1 heaped teaspoon ground coriander
1 heaped teaspoon paprika

Preheat your oven to its highest setting. Line a large baking tray with baking paper.

Place the pepper halves skin side up on the prepared baking tray and roast for about 12–14 minutes, or until nicely charred. Remove from the oven, turn the peppers over and leave them to cool.

Using a sharp knife, cut a disc of peel off the top and base of each orange in turn, then, working from the top of the fruit downwards, cut away the remaining peel and pith in strips until the entire orange is peeled. Slice each orange widthways into 4 or 5 slices and then cut the slices in half into semicircles.

Mix the dressing ingredients together in a jug or small bowl and season well with salt and pepper.

Once the peppers have cooled, place them in a bowl, pour the dressing over and toss to coat.

Arrange the chicory, oranges and peppers on a large platter and then top with the anchovies. Sprinkle over the pine nuts and season with salt and pepper before serving.

SIMPLY DELICIOUS WITH…

Fragrant Fish Cakes with Preserved Lemon Mayonnaise (see page 152) and Crispy Cod Wraps with Salsa & Harissa Lime Mayo (see page 160).

Smoked aubergine, tomato, tamarind & peanut salad

Smoking aubergines is such a classic Middle Eastern technique, but this recipe is quite different to any other, and I must confess that the first time I made it, I ate the whole lot! Any recipe that has texture and a combination of savoury, sweet and sour is always a winner in my view. I like simple dishes that burst with flavour, and this does just that.

SERVES 6—8

4 aubergines

3 large tomatoes, each cut into 6, or 10 cherry tomatoes, halved

2 tablespoons caster sugar

1 heaped tablespoon unsweetened tamarind paste

1 tablespoon vegan red wine vinegar

2 shallots, halved and thinly sliced into half moons

2 tablespoons olive oil

2 generous handfuls of salted peanuts, roughly chopped

Maldon sea salt flakes and freshly ground black pepper

Using tongs, blister and char the aubergines either on a barbecue or over the flame of a gas hob, blackening the skins all over and cooking them until they have collapsed in size by half.

Place the aubergines on a heatproof surface or tray and leave to cool for about 20 minutes until they are cool enough for you to handle. Keeping the stalks intact, split the aubergines lengthways in half and use a large metal spoon to scoop out all the flesh into a fine-mesh sieve to drain off the excess juices, discarding the charred skins.

Once drained, tip the aubergine flesh into a mixing bowl, add the remaining ingredients, except the olive oil and peanuts, and use a fork to mix together thoroughly. Season generously with salt and pepper to taste, then add the olive oil and mix well. Finally, stir in the peanuts and serve. This salad is great served as part of a feast or with barbecued meats.

SIMPLY DELICIOUS WITH...

Tepsi Kebap (see page 84) or Lamb, Cumin, Coriander & Chilli Kebabs (see page 118).

TIP

If using a gas hob to char the aubergines, line your hob with foil to avoid a messy clear-up job.

Spiced pork stew

When slow-cooked, pork shoulder falls apart and the fat it contains means it remains juicy. Pork can really stand up to spices, and while it may not be a looker, this boldly spiced stew is a comfort staple of mine. The longer you cook it, the more the meat falls apart, and it's so versatile – you can eat it with rice or bread, or pile on to a jacket potato. You can add beans to the leftovers or use it as a filling for a wrap or even a pie, and it freezes well, too.

SERVES 4—6

vegetable oil

2 onions, finely chopped

1kg boneless pork shoulder, cut into 4cm chunks

3 tablespoons medium curry powder

1 tablespoon garlic granules

1 tablespoon paprika

1 tablespoon ground coriander

1 tablespoon celery salt

2 heaped teaspoons ground allspice

4–5 sprigs of thyme, leaves picked

6 fat garlic cloves, thinly sliced

1 Scotch bonnet chilli, pierced but left whole

4 tomatoes, roughly diced

4 spring onions, thinly sliced

Maldon sea salt flakes, if needed, and freshly ground black pepper

naan bread, or rice and peas, to serve

Place a large saucepan over a medium-high heat and pour in enough vegetable oil to coat the base of the pan. Add the onions and cook for a few minutes until softened and translucent, without browning.

Add the pork, curry powder, garlic granules, paprika, coriander, celery salt, allspice, thyme and a generous amount of pepper and stir until the meat is well coated in the seasonings, then add the garlic slices, Scotch bonnet chilli, tomatoes and spring onions and mix well. Pour over enough cold water to cover the ingredients, stir and reduce the heat to medium-low. Cook the stew, uncovered, for 15 minutes, then stir, cover the pan with a lid and continue to cook for a minimum of 4 hours (I cook it for 6 hours on a gentle heat for the best results), ensuring you stir it every now and again. One hour before the end of the cooking time, check and adjust the seasoning and, if necessary, add just enough water to create a sauce-like consistency. If after 3 hours' cooking there is a lot of liquid in the pan, remove the lid for the last hour of cooking to reduce. Remove the chilli, then serve with naan bread or plain boiled rice and peas.

Spice-seared lamb
with courgette ribbons, pickled chillies & pine nuts

This perfect summer salad has sharp bursts of flavour from the preserved lemons and pickled chillies in the dressing, and can easily be scaled up to feed a crowd. You can even cook the lamb on the barbecue and make the salad ahead – just assemble it all before serving.

SERVES 6–8

50g pine nuts

1 teaspoon fennel seeds

1 teaspoon cumin seeds

1 teaspoon coriander seeds

olive oil

500g lamb steaks, 1cm thick
  (about 3–4 steaks)

2 small courgettes

4 pickled chillies, thinly sliced

4 preserved lemons, deseeded and
  finely chopped

4–5 sprigs of parsley, leaves picked

Maldon sea salt flakes and freshly
  ground black pepper

Preheat the oven to 200°C, Gas Mark 6. Place the pine nuts in a baking dish and toast in the oven for 6 minutes until golden, then set aside.

Place a frying pan over a medium-high heat. Add the fennel, cumin and coriander seeds and toast them, shaking the pan, for 2 minutes until they release their aroma. Transfer the toasted seeds to a pestle and mortar and finely grind, then leave to cool. Place the pan back on the heat.

Drizzle 2 tablespoons olive oil over the lamb, add the ground spices and work them into the meat until the steaks are evenly coated with the spice mix. Season both sides with pepper and then sear each steak in the hot frying pan for 1 minute on each side, sprinkling each side with just a little salt, until nicely browned. Remove from the pan and leave to rest.

Using a vegetable peeler, cut the courgettes lengthways in long, thin ribbons into a mixing bowl. Drizzle with 2–3 tablespoons olive oil, then add a generous amount of pepper, the pickled chillies, preserved lemon, parsley and toasted pine nuts and mix together well. Arrange on serving plates. Slice the lamb steaks, lay on top of the salad and serve immediately.

SIMPLY DELICIOUS WITH...

Watermelon, Black Olive & Feta with Cayenne, Honey & Lime Dressing (see page 143).

TIP
Toasting the pine nuts in the oven, rather than in a frying pan, ensures even toasting.

Marinated steak
with labneh, pul biber butter & crispy onions

Taking inspiration from the Iskender kebap of Turkey, this dish of marinated steak with labneh (or strained yogurt, if you prefer) and pul biber butter is a simple yet effective explosion of flavours. Swipe pillowy flatbread through the yogurt for maximum enjoyment.

SERVES 4—6

450–500g sirloin steak, 2cm thick, trimmed of excess fat and cut into 2.5cm cubes

1 heaped tablespoon dried mint

1 teaspoon garlic granules

1 teaspoon ground cumin

½ teaspoon celery salt

2 tablespoons olive oil

75g butter

2 heaped teaspoons pul biber chilli flakes

400g labneh, or Greek yogurt strained in a muslin bag overnight (see method on page 11)

generous handful of shop-bought crispy fried onions

2–3 sprigs of dill, very finely chopped

Maldon sea salt flakes and freshly ground black pepper

Ensure the steak is at room temperature before cooking.

Put the steak cubes into a mixing bowl with the dried mint, garlic granules, cumin, celery salt and a generous amount of pepper and mix together well. Pour in the olive oil and mix again. Leave the meat to marinate for about 10 minutes while you heat a large frying pan over a medium-high heat.

Add the meat cubes to the hot pan and cook for 1 minute on each side, then transfer to a small plate and season with salt. Turn off the heat and wipe the frying pan with kitchen paper. Return the pan to a low heat and add the butter. Once melted, add the pul biber and stir a little until the butter turns red from the pul biber, then remove the pan from the heat.

Spread out the labneh or strained Greek yogurt on a large plate. Lift the steak off the plate using a slotted spoon and shake off the excess juices, then arrange on the labneh or yogurt before pouring the spiced butter over the steak. Scatter over the crispy onions followed by the dill and serve immediately.

SIMPLY DELICIOUS WITH...
Ultimate Falafels (see page 81) or Polow-e-Bademjan-o-Felfel (see page 125).

Spiced beef pancakes
with chopped egg, dill & crème fraîche

Whenever I think of pancakes or Pancake Day (Shrove Tuesday), I rarely think of sweet combinations, unlike many people, and I must admit that I will always choose savoury over sweet dishes. These pancakes combine some of my favourite ingredients in every mouthful, and what is really lovely about them is how convivial they are, ideal for feasting and sharing where everyone can make their own combinations and enjoy them without you having to plate them up individually.

MAKES 6

4 eggs
vegetable oil, for frying
500g minced beef
1 tablespoon garlic granules
1 tablespoon ground cumin
1 tablespoon paprika
½ teaspoon cayenne pepper
½ teaspoon ground cinnamon
2 shallots, very finely chopped
1 small packet (about 30g) of fresh
    dill, finely chopped

150g crème fraîche
Maldon sea salt flakes and freshly ground
    black pepper

FOR THE PANCAKES

50g plain flour
pinch of salt
1 egg
100ml milk
25ml water
25g salted butter, melted

Pour boiling water from a kettle into a saucepan set over a medium-high heat. Once the water is bubbling, carefully lower in the eggs and boil for 10 minutes. Drain the eggs and place them under cold running water to stop the cooking process, then leave them to cool in cold water until needed.

Place a large frying pan over a medium-high heat, drizzle in a little vegetable oil and add the minced beef. Immediately begin breaking the meat up as finely as you can to avoid clumps. Once the meat has cooked a little, stir in the garlic granules, spices and a generous amount of pepper. Continue cooking the meat until it is well browned, then season generously with salt, mix well and remove the pan from the heat.

CONTINUED OVERLEAF

To make the pancakes, preheat the oven to 180°C (160°C fan), Gas Mark 4. Line an ovenproof dish with greaseproof paper.

Put the flour, salt and egg into a large mixing bowl. Mix the milk and water together in a jug, then blend into the flour mixture a little at a time, whisking well to beat out any lumps. Mix in the melted butter, then transfer to a measuring jug. Place an 18cm frying pan over a medium-high heat and drizzle in a tiny amount of vegetable oil. Once the oil is hot, ladle in just enough of the batter to make a thin pancake and cook for about 1 minute on each side, or until nicely browned. Transfer to the prepared dish, cover with foil and place in the oven to keep warm while you make the rest of the pancakes.

Shell the hard-boiled eggs and finely chop them, then place in a little bowl, along with the shallots, dill and crème fraîche in separate small bowls.

Briefly reheat the beef mixture over a high heat, and once hot, divide it between the pancakes. Top with the egg, shallots, dill and, finally, a good dollop of crème fraîche before serving.

Green & black-eyed bean baklava
with feta & honey

I absolutely love a savoury baklava. Technically, it's just a pie sweetened with a drizzle of syrup, although in this recipe laziness prevailed and I switched from my usual syrup to clear honey, which means it's even easier to make. This is one of those perfect all-in-one meals that doesn't need any accompaniment. However, if you really insist, then a crisp green salad on the side would be the ideal partner.

SERVES 8

olive oil

2 onions, halved and thinly sliced
   into half moons

6 fat garlic cloves, thinly sliced

400g trimmed fine green beans,
   halved in length

3 tablespoons tomato purée

1 teaspoon ground turmeric

1 teaspoon ground cinnamon

1 teaspoon paprika

400g can chopped tomatoes

2 tablespoons caster sugar

100ml cold water

400g can black-eyed beans, drained
   reserving half the brine

25g butter, plus an extra 50g butter,
   melted, for brushing

6 sheets of filo pastry (each about
   48 x 25cm)

200g vegetarian feta cheese, crumbled

Maldon sea salt flakes and freshly
   ground black pepper

clear honey, to serve

Place a large saucepan over a medium heat and pour in enough olive oil to coat the base of the pan. Add the onions and cook for a few minutes until softened and translucent, without browning. Add the garlic and cook, stirring, for 2 minutes, then add the green beans, turn the heat up slightly and cook until they soften, stirring regularly.

Add the tomato purée, turmeric, cinnamon and paprika and stir until the vegetable mixture is well coated, then add the canned tomatoes, the brine from the beans and the sugar and stir well. Pour in the water and stir again, then reduce the heat to medium-low and simmer for 20 minutes. Remove the pan from the heat, add the black-eyed beans, stir through the 25g butter, season with salt and pepper, then leave to rest and cool completely.

CONTINUED OVERLEAF

Meanwhile, preheat the oven to 200°C (180°C fan), Gas Mark 6.

Select a rectangular ovenproof dish, about 32 x 22cm, and brush the base liberally with some of the melted butter. Line the base of the dish with 4 sheets of filo pastry – 2 lengthways and 2 widthways – allowing an equal amount of pastry to overhang each side of the dish. Brush the pastry with melted butter. Pour in the green and black-eyed bean mixture and shake the dish to create an even layer, then scatter the feta on top.

Fold the overhanging pastry over the filling. Take the remaining pastry sheets, fold them so they are slightly larger than the dish, then place them over the filling to cover the top. Tuck the pastry edges down the sides of the dish using a round-bladed knife or similar so the top looks neat and smooth, then brush the top liberally with the remaining melted butter. Using a very sharp knife, cut the top layer of pastry into 8 equal portions (this makes it easier to portion once cooked), then bake for 30–35 minutes until deep golden brown.

Remove from the oven, cut the baklava along the scored lines into portions and drizzle each portion with a little honey, as liked, then serve.

SIMPLY DELICIOUS WITH...
Green-yogurt-dressed Baby Gem Lettuce with Burnt Hazelnuts (see page 44).

Chargrilled saffron squid with chilli & charred lemons

Chargrilled squid always reminds me of summer holidays in the Mediterranean. Every time I cook it, I wonder why I don't make it more often, as there is nothing fiddly involved. The crispy garlic, charred chilli and the juice from the charred lemons in this recipe turn this dish into something truly spectacular and flavour-packed.

SERVES 4

vegetable oil, for frying

4 garlic cloves, thinly sliced

8 frozen squid tubes (about 400g total weight), defrosted

2 pinches of saffron threads

2 lemons, halved

2 long red chillies

50g rocket leaves

olive oil, for drizzling

Maldon sea salt flakes and black pepper

Line a plate with a double layer of kitchen paper. Pour enough vegetable oil into a small saucepan to fill to a depth of about 1cm. Add the garlic slices and fry over a medium-low heat for a few minutes until lightly golden (avoid browning as they will taste bitter). Remove with a slotted spoon and transfer to the paper-lined plate to drain.

Using a sharp knife, cut down one side of each squid tube and open it out flat on the chopping board with the outside facing up. Score the outside flesh gently in diagonal lines about 1cm apart, first in one direction and then in the opposite direction, to create a diamond pattern. Cut in half so that you get 2 pieces from each squid body. Place all the squid pieces in a small bowl or food bag, crumble in the saffron and rub into the squid. Cover the bowl with clingfilm or seal the bag and leave to marinate in the refrigerator for 1 hour.

Heat a nonstick griddle pan over a high heat. Once hot, chargrill the squid for 2–3 minutes on each side, then remove from the pan and transfer to a plate. Add the chillies and lemons, cut side down, and cook, turning the chillies frequently until charred all over. Arrange the rocket on plates with the chargrilled squid pieces, then thinly slice the charred chillies and scatter over. Drizzle with olive oil, season with salt and pepper, scatter with the fried garlic slices and serve with the charred lemon halves.

SIMPLY DELICIOUS WITH…

Cauliflower & Asparagus Black Rice Salad (see page 174) or Harissa Kofta Lettuce Cups (see page 123).

Firecracker prawns

I absolutely love prawns and they would most definitely be part of my ideal meal. And the larger they are, the more I love them. The first time I made this recipe I managed to find the most enormous prawns, which made the finished dish utterly spectacular. But I recommend only using what is easy for you to get hold of, and yes, if you don't like the shells, you can use peeled prawns, although go for the very best quality you can find. The sauce is punchy, fiery, fruity and aromatic – everything I love. A little rice on the side or even some bread to mop up the juices would complete the picture.

SERVES 4–6

2 unwaxed oranges

2–3 tablespoons olive oil

4 fat garlic cloves, thinly sliced

10cm piece of fresh root ginger, peeled and finely grated

8 large uncooked prawns in their shells, about 70g each (or use 12 smaller ones)

3 tablespoons Sriracha

generous handful of marjoram leaves (or use 1 tablespoon dried marjoram if that's all you can find), plus extra to garnish

25g salted butter

Maldon sea salt flakes and freshly ground black pepper

Using a vegetable peeler, peel the rind of the oranges, then slice into thin strips. Squeeze and reserve the juice.

Heat your largest frying pan or a wok over a high heat. Once hot, add the olive oil, quickly followed by the garlic and ginger, and stir-fry for a few seconds without letting them burn. Add the prawns and toss them in the garlic and ginger. When they begin to cook (the cooking time will vary depending on the size of prawns you use, but look for them to turn pinkish white), stir in the orange rind strips, then add the Sriracha and orange juice. Stir until the prawns are well coated in the mixture, then season well with salt and pepper and add the marjoram.

Cook the sauce for several minutes, stirring if necessary to avoid the prawns catching, until it is reduced and turns sticky and the prawns are cooked through. Stir in the butter, and once melted, turn the prawns one last time to coat in the sauce before serving immediately, garnished with extra marjoram leaves if liked.

SIMPLY DELICIOUS WITH...

Tomato & Garlic Rice (see page 38) or Adas Polow (see page 101).

Chard, ricotta & runny egg pie

This pie brings several of my loves together: bitter greens, cheese and a good runny egg.
If you can't find chard, use spinach, rocket or your favourite leafy greens.

SERVES 6—8

olive oil

400g chard, stalks thinly sliced and
   leaves roughly chopped

200g cabbage leaves or spring greens,
   stalks removed and leaves roughly
   shredded

2 tablespoons garlic granules

1 tablespoon ground coriander

1 heaped tablespoon sumac

500g ricotta cheese

75g butter, melted

7 sheets of filo pastry (each about
   48 x 25cm)

6 eggs

1 teaspoon nigella seeds

Maldon sea salt flakes and freshly
   ground black pepper

Place a large saucepan over a medium heat, and pour in enough olive oil to coat the base of the
pan. Add the chard stalks and cook for a few minutes until softened, then add the leaves and
cabbage and stir-fry for a few minutes until beginning to soften. Add the garlic granules and
coriander and cook for several minutes, stirring occasionally, until the leaves are wilted and
cooked through. Season very generously (the mixture will need over-seasoning at this stage)
and stir well, then add the sumac and mix until well combined. Leave to cool.

Preheat the oven to 200°C (180°C fan), Gas Mark 6.

Fold the ricotta into the cooled greens mixture and check and adjust the seasoning.

Select an ovenproof dish, about 32 x 22cm, and brush the base liberally with melted butter.
Line the base of the dish with 4 sheets of filo pastry – 2 lengthways and 2 widthways – allowing
an equal amount of pastry to overhang each side of the dish. Brush the top layer with melted
butter. Pour the ricotta mixture over and spread it out into an even layer. Make 6 holes in the
mixture and crack an egg into each. Season the eggs with a little pepper, then gently lay a pastry
sheet over to cover the entire filling. Fold the overhanging pastry over the filling and lightly
brush the edges with more melted butter. Cut the remaining 2 pastry sheets in half, crumple
up each piece and arrange them on top of the pie. Brush generously with the remaining melted
butter and sprinkle with nigella seeds.

Bake the pie for 20–25 minutes until golden brown. For well-cooked eggs, lower the oven
temperature to 180°C (160°C fan), Gas Mark 4, and cook for a further 30 minutes.

Grilled pineapple & potato kari

One of the joys of spices is that they perfectly complement anything containing a little sweetness, giving your palate a pleasing balance. A little acidity never goes amiss when pairing spice with sweet, and this curry hits all those notes beautifully. It may feel a little adventurous for some to combine fruit with stews and curries, but it's nothing new – many cultures have been doing it for centuries and for good reason, as it's absolutely delicious!

SERVES 6

2 tablespoons vegetable oil, plus extra
    for brushing

1 teaspoon cumin seeds

1 teaspoon fennel seeds

1 teaspoon black mustard seeds

1 large onion, roughly chopped

1 teaspoon ground cinnamon

1 teaspoon ground turmeric

1–2 small green chillies, split
    lengthways but kept whole

400g can chopped tomatoes

500g baby new potatoes

1 large pineapple

Maldon sea salt flakes and freshly
    ground black pepper

rice or flatbreads, to serve

Place a large saucepan over a medium heat, pour in 2 tablespoons vegetable oil and add all the seeds. Once they sizzle, add the onion and cook for a few minutes until softened, then stir in the cinnamon, turmeric, a generous amount of salt and pepper and the chillies and cook for 1 minute.

Add the canned tomatoes, then fill the can with cold water, pour into the pan and stir. Bring to the boil and add the potatoes whole (if they are large, cut them into 3cm chunks before adding). Stir well, then reduce the heat and simmer for about 30–35 minutes until the potatoes are cooked through, adding a little more water or covering the pan with a lid to maintain the liquid level.

Meanwhile, peel and core the pineapple, then cut the flesh into 4cm chunks. Heat a nonstick griddle pan over a high heat. Brush each pineapple chunk with a little oil, add to the hot pan and cook them for 1 minute on each side until charred.

Once the potatoes in the curry are cooked, remove the chillies, add the charred pineapple pieces to the curry, stir and heat through, then serve with rice or flatbreads.

SIMPLY DELICIOUS WITH...

Flame-roasted Pepper, Pistachio & Dill Yogurt (see page 42) or Chargrilled Aubergines (see page 140).

Red kidney bean & sweet potato stew *with yogurt & hot mint oil*

The yogurt in this vegetarian stew is a perfect, cooling contrast, and the hot mint oil – a very Persian addition we call *nana daagh* – finishes the dish incredibly well. You can serve this with rice or bread, and leftovers make an excellent brunch dish with poached eggs.

SERVES 4—6

vegetable oil, for frying

1 large onion, diced

4 fat garlic cloves, thinly sliced

2 teaspoons cumin seeds

1 teaspoon ground cinnamon

1 teaspoon ground turmeric

1 teaspoon chilli flakes

690g (1 large jar) passata

500g sweet potato, peeled and cut into 1cm chunks

400g can red kidney beans, drained

1 small packet (about 30g) of flat leaf parsley, roughly chopped

1 tablespoon dried mint

150g Greek yogurt

Maldon sea salt flakes and freshly ground black pepper

Place a large saucepan over a medium heat and pour in enough oil to coat the base of the pan. Add the onion and cook for a few minutes until it begins to turn translucent, then add the garlic, stirring to ensure it doesn't burn. Continue cooking until both have softened, without browning. Add the spices and coat the onion mixture in them, then cook, stirring, for a minute or so. Season generously with salt and with pepper to taste, then stir in the passata. Reduce the heat to low and simmer gently, uncovered, for about 25 minutes.

Stir the sweet potato into the stew and cook for a further 20 minutes or so until the sweet potato is tender, then add the beans and most of the parsley and heat through.

Place a separate pan over a medium heat, add the dried mint and 1 tablespoon of vegetable oil and heat the mint for a few minutes, without letting it burn. Remove the pan from the heat.

Transfer the stew to bowls, add dollops of the yogurt around the dish and scatter over the remaining parsley, then pour over the hot mint oil and serve immediately.

SIMPLY DELICIOUS WITH...

Adas Polow (see page 101).

Goats' cheese, vegetable & za'atar filo tart

Think of this as a sort of quiche but with a filo pastry base instead – the perfect match for the rich, creamy goats' cheese filling, spiked with the heady fragrance of za'atar.

SERVES 6—8

vegetable oil

1 aubergine, finely diced

1 red pepper, cored, deseeded and
    finely diced

1 courgette, finely diced

50g butter, melted

6 sheets of filo pastry (each about
    48 x 25cm)

7 eggs, 1 beaten, to glaze

300ml double cream

2 tablespoons za'atar

1 teaspoon garlic granules

250g rindless soft goats' cheese,
    torn into rough chunks

Maldon sea salt flakes and black pepper

Preheat the oven to 200°C (180°C fan), Gas Mark 6.

Line a tray with a double layer of kitchen paper. Place a large saucepan over a high heat and pour in enough vegetable oil to coat the base of the pan. Add the aubergine, mix with the oil and cook for several minutes until it begins to brown, stirring occasionally. Add the red pepper and cook for a few minutes until softened. Finally, add the courgette and cook for 6–8 minutes, stirring occasionally. Remove the vegetables with a slotted spoon, shaking off any excess oil, then transfer to the paper-lined tray to drain and leave to cool.

Meanwhile, select an ovenproof dish, about 32 x 22cm. Brush melted butter over each pastry sheet and lay 2 layers lengthways in the dish with the ends overhanging the short edges of the dish. Take the remaining 4 sheets and lay 2 layers side by side widthways across the dish so that they meet in the centre, with the excess overhanging the long edges of the dish. Crumple the overhanging pastry inside the edges of the dish to create a border for your pie, leaving room for the filling. Brush the crumpled pastry with the beaten egg.

Beat the remaining 6 eggs and fold in the cream, za'atar and garlic granules, followed by the cooked vegetables. Season with salt and pepper. Pour the mixture into the filo base, scatter over the goats' cheese and bake for 30 minutes until golden brown.

SIMPLY DELICIOUS WITH...

Pear, Chickpea & Green Leaf Salad with Maple Harissa Dressing (see page 172).

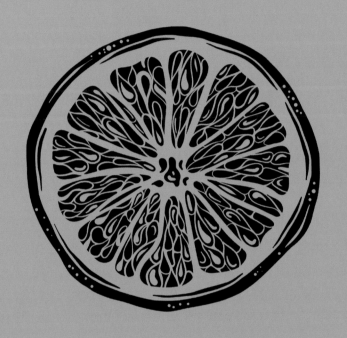

Cakes, bakes & sweet treats

Stuffed dates
with torched goats' cheese, pistachios & honey

Dates are very important in Middle Eastern culture, but I've only ever really enjoyed them when married with something savoury. Here, the slightly acidic yet creamy, mild soft goats' cheese is the perfect pairing, along with a little drizzle of honey and the satisfying crunch of the king of Persian nuts – the wonderful pistachio.

MAKES 12

12 large dates
250g rindless soft goats' cheese
1 generous tablespoon clear honey
25g pistachio slivers (or whole nuts,
    finely blitzed in a food processor
    or very finely chopped)

Using a sharp knife, carefully cut along one side of each date in turn, open out and remove the stone, but be careful to avoid splitting them in half.

Cut the goats' cheese into 12 equal portions, about 20g each. Roll each portion into a ball and then elongate into a sausage shape that will fit snugly into the cavities of the dates. Fill all the dates with the goats' cheese, place on a plate and put into the freezer for 20 minutes to firm up.

Remove from the freezer. Using a small kitchen blowtorch, run the flame over the cheese-filled area of each stuffed date for a few seconds until slightly charred. Arrange all the dates on a platter, drizzle with a very thin stream of honey, scatter with the pistachios and serve with a nice cup of black tea infused with mint leaves.

Barberry fool

If you're in need of a foolproof, super-quick dessert, then this is the one. While Persians never use barberries in desserts, I am an experimenter and one who likes to get the best from the ingredients I buy. Barberries have a wonderfully sour nature that makes them incredibly versatile in cooking, marinades, butter compounds and even drinks… so why not in a dessert? This is one of those ridiculously easy recipes that's a perfect quick fix for when you want a sweet treat but prefer to put all the effort into making the savouries instead.

SERVES 6

50g dried barberries, plus extra
    to decorate
4 tablespoons boiling water
600ml double cream
6 tablespoons icing sugar
4 tablespoons Greek yogurt
handful of pistachio slivers
    (or very roughly chopped
    whole nuts), to decorate

Put the barberries into a heatproof mixing bowl, pour over the boiling water and leave to soak for a few minutes.

Transfer the barberries and their soaking liquid to a blender and blitz to a paste.

Using an electric hand whisk, whip the cream with the icing sugar in a large mixing bowl until stiff peaks form, then gently fold in the barberry paste and Greek yogurt.

Serve in individual glasses, and decorate with a few extra barberries and the pistachios.

Lime & black pepper frozen yogurt

Why I didn't think of this recipe years ago is beyond me. Simply put, if you want something to refresh your palate after a heavy meal and give you just a hint of sweetness and plenty of satisfaction, then this is for you. It's probably the most surprising little sorbet you could try – it sounds like it shouldn't work but it really, really does and I love it so much that I could happily eat it every day, especially when the weather is warmer.

SERVES 4

500g Greek yogurt
60g icing sugar
finely grated zest and juice of
    1 fat unwaxed lime
1 teaspoon freshly ground
    black pepper

Put all the ingredients into a mixing bowl and mix together well.

Pour the yogurt mixture into an ice-cream maker and churn according to the manufacturer's instructions.

This frozen yogurt is best served straight from the ice-cream maker.

Roasted walnut & tahini ice cream

This ice cream is truly something else. I find myself eating it even before it's fully set. It really is at its peak when it just comes out of the ice-cream maker – set, but still soft and gooey enough to eat spoon after spoon.

SERVES 4—6

150g walnuts

300ml milk

300ml double cream

4 tablespoons tahini

100g caster sugar

3 large egg yolks

Preheat the oven to 200°C (180°C fan), Gas Mark 6.

Spread the walnuts out on a baking tray and toast in the oven for 10–12 minutes. Remove from the oven and leave to cool. Pulse the cooled walnuts briefly in a food processor (or roughly chop) to retain some texture rather than finely grinding them, then set aside.

Heat the milk and cream gently in a saucepan over a low heat until warm, then add the tahini and mix well until it has dissolved. Add half the sugar and stir until dissolved, then remove the pan from the heat and leave to cool.

Put the egg yolks and remaining sugar into a mixing bowl and whisk together using an electric hand whisk until pale and thickened. Slowly pour in a little of the cooled cream mixture, stirring as you go to ensure it is quickly incorporated, then add the remaining cream mixture and mix well. Pour the entire mixture back into the pan and heat gently over a low heat until it almost comes to the boil, then remove the pan from the heat. The custard should be thick enough to coat the back of a spoon. Cool the custard (you can speed this process up by pouring it into a glass bowl and placing the bowl on to ice or into very cold water), stirring occasionally.

Once the custard is completely cold, stir in the chopped walnuts, then pour into an ice-cream maker and churn for about 1 hour. You can serve the ice cream immediately or, if you prefer a firmer texture, transfer it to a freezerproof container and freeze for later use. If serving from the freezer, leave to stand at room temperature for 20 minutes to allow it to soften slightly.

Apple, poppy seed & lemon loaf cake

God knows I love cake. But although it is one of my great loves, I exercise a great deal of moderation and it really does have to be a very good cake in order for me to indulge. Loaf cakes are one of my favourite things to bake – simple, versatile and no tricky fiddling or sandwiching of layers. You can add icings, vary the ingredients and use up whatever you have without needing large quantities of anything, which is how this recipe came about. Sometimes when I buy apples and they are a bit lacking in crunch, I prefer to make a cake rather than eat them as is. I like my cakes to be moist and fruity with lots of different flavours, and this example ticks all the boxes. Warm it up and it's great with custard or ice cream, too.

SERVES 8–10

3 very small or 2 medium apples (I use Braeburn), quartered

3 eggs

175g caster sugar

finely grated zest of 2 unwaxed lemons

1 teaspoon vanilla bean paste

½ teaspoon almond extract

175g plain flour

1 teaspoon baking powder

150g unsalted butter, melted

1 heaped tablespoon poppy seeds, plus a little extra for sprinkling over the top

Preheat the oven to 180°C (160°C fan), Gas Mark 4. Line a 900g loaf tin with a nonstick paper liner or baking paper.

Core the apples, keeping the skins on, and then finely dice.

Put the eggs, sugar, lemon zest, vanilla bean paste and almond extract into a mixing bowl and beat together until well combined. Add the flour, baking powder and melted butter and mix again. Gently fold in the apples, without crushing them too much, and the poppy seeds.

Pour the batter into the prepared loaf tin and sprinkle the top with extra poppy seeds. Bake the cake for 50 minutes–1 hour (my own oven takes an hour), or until cooked through and a skewer or knife inserted into the centre of the cake comes out clean. Remove from the oven, turn the cake out of the tin on to a wire rack and leave to cool before serving.

Saffron & sesame shortbreads

I absolutely love shortbread. The buttery, crumbly goodness of it makes it the master of all biscuits in my humble opinion. The saffron-tinted Persian biscuits of the patisseries in my neighbourhood when I was growing up provided the inspiration for this combination. But while I have enjoyed many Persian sweet treats, they really aren't a patch on the marvellous shortbread biscuit, so here it is uniquely flavoured with saffron and sesame – perfect with a cup of sweetened black tea, which is just how we like it.

MAKES 18—20

100g sesame seeds

250g plain flour

100g icing sugar

generous pinch of Maldon sea salt flakes

200g unsalted butter, softened

0.5g (½ teaspoon) saffron threads, ground to a powder using a pestle and mortar, then steeped in 1 tablespoon boiling water until cool

caster sugar, for sprinkling

Preheat the oven to 220°C (200°C fan), Gas Mark 7.

Spread the sesame seeds out on a baking tray and toast for 6–8 minutes until browned. Remove from the oven and leave to cool.

Combine the sesame seeds with the flour, icing sugar, salt and butter in a mixing bowl, then add the saffron solution and work the ingredients into a dough.

Divide the dough in half and form each half into a sausage about 4–5cm in diameter. Wrap each sausage in clingfilm and twist the ends to tightly encase the dough, like a sweet wrapper. Refrigerate for 1 hour. Alternatively, you can freeze them for another day.

Preheat the oven to 170°C (150°C fan), Gas Mark 3½. Line a large baking tray with baking paper. Unwrap each sausage of dough, then cut into 1cm-thick slices and lay on the prepared baking tray about 2cm apart. Bake for 20 minutes. Remove from the oven and sprinkle with caster sugar. Leave to cool on the tray before serving.

Pistachio, lemon & rosemary cake

The pistachio is the king of Persian nuts, and using naturally bright green Persian pistachio slivers helps create the electric green colour of this cake. Fragrant with lemon zest and aromatic rosemary, it's also gluten free.

SERVES 8–10

150g unsalted butter

4 x 10cm sprigs of rosemary, leaves
very finely chopped

3 eggs

100g golden caster sugar

1 teaspoon vanilla extract

1 teaspoon lemon extract (alcohol-free)

2 heaped tablespoons Greek yogurt

finely grated zest of 3 large unwaxed
lemons

100g ground almonds

300g pistachio slivers (or whole nuts),
very finely blitzed in a food
processor, plus extra to decorate

FOR THE ICING

150g icing sugar

25ml freshly squeezed lemon juice

Preheat the oven to 180°C (160°C fan), Gas Mark 4. Take a large square of baking paper, scrunch it up, then smooth it out and use to line a 22–24cm round cake tin or ovenproof dish.

Warm the butter in a saucepan over a gentle heat until just melted, then remove from the heat, stir in the rosemary and leave to infuse.

Put the eggs, caster sugar and vanilla and lemon extracts into a mixing bowl and beat together until well combined. Mix in the yogurt, followed by most of the lemon zest (reserving a little for decorating the cake), the ground almonds and pistachios. Pour in the infused melted butter and mix again until evenly combined.

Pour the batter into the prepared cake tin or ovenproof dish and shake to level the surface, then bake for about 45 minutes until golden brown on top and springy to touch. Remove from the oven and leave the cake to cool completely in the tin or dish.

Mix the icing ingredients together in a small bowl until smooth.

Carefully remove the cake from the tin or dish and set it on a serving plate. Pour the icing on top and leave to set, then scatter with the pistachios and reserved lemon zest before serving.

Tahini, almond & orange brownies

These almond-based orange-spiked brownies are so good, simple to make and even gluten free to boot. I absolutely love combining chocolate and orange in cakes and desserts, as they work so well together, but the nuts and the wonderfully rich tahini really crank up the flavour while also keeping these little brownie squares lovely and soft.

MAKES 9 OR 12

4 eggs

200g caster sugar

1 tablespoon natural vanilla extract

finely grated zest and juice of

   2 unwaxed oranges

4 heaped tablespoons cocoa powder

400g ground almonds

200g salted butter, melted

4 heaped tablespoons tahini of

   pouring consistency, thinned

   with warm water if necessary

100g dark chocolate chunks or chips

   (70% cocoa solids)

Preheat the oven to 180°C (160°C fan), Gas Mark 4. Line a 20cm square cake tin with baking paper, ensuring the paper comes up a little over the sides.

Beat the eggs, sugar and vanilla extract together in a large mixing bowl until combined. Add the orange zest and juice and cocoa powder and mix well. Add the ground almonds, then stir in the melted butter. Add the runny tahini and really work it well into the mixture – it will stiffen a little, so add a tablespoon of warm water if it seizes too much. Finally, fold in the chocolate.

Pour the batter into the prepared tin and then shake the tin and tap it on the work surface to settle the mixture evenly. Bake for 45–50 minutes, or until cooked through and a skewer or knife inserted into the centre of the brownie comes out clean. Remove from the oven, then use the paper to lift the brownie out of the tin. Leave to cool on a wire rack on the paper, then cut into squares.

TIP

These brownies are really good served with custard.

Blueberry, pistachio & coconut cake

There is so much flavour on every level here: chewy, nutty, fruity, zesty, cakey goodness… I'm fairly sure that's all I need to tell you to send you looking for your loaf tin. If, by some small miracle, you are a nerd like I am and own two loaf tins, do yourself the kindness of doubling the batch and baking two cakes at once. I made friends with my new neighbours by dropping off one of these cakes at their door – the best lesson in life I've ever learned is that you'll always win friends with cake.

SERVES 8—10

3 eggs
150g caster sugar
1 teaspoon vanilla bean paste
1 teaspoon almond extract
1 teaspoon lemon extract (alcohol-free)
50g desiccated coconut
175g unsalted butter, melted
175g plain flour
1 teaspoon baking powder
4 tablespoons milk
generous handful of pistachio nuts
200g blueberries

Preheat the oven to 170°C (150°C fan), Gas Mark 3½. Line a 900g loaf tin with a nonstick paper liner or baking paper.

Put the eggs, sugar, vanilla bean paste and almond and lemon extracts into a large mixing bowl and beat together until well combined. Add the coconut and mix well, then stir in the melted butter until incorporated. Add the flour, baking powder and milk and mix until smooth. Finally, stir in the pistachios, then gently fold in the blueberries.

Pour the batter into the prepared loaf tin and bake for about 1 hour, or until cooked through and a skewer or knife inserted into the centre of the cake comes out clean. Remove from the oven, turn the cake out of the tin on to a wire rack and leave to cool. Serve in slices with a nice cup of tea.

White chocolate, raspberry & pistachio tiramisu

A classic tiramisu is one dessert I can rarely resist, but this recipe offers stiff competition – white chocolate and raspberries are made for each other, and the vibrant green pistachios add a nutty flourish that makes this dish the absolutely perfect way to round off a meal.

SERVES 6—8

100g white chocolate, broken into pieces

400g raspberries

2 teaspoons icing sugar

3 tablespoons cold water

2 eggs, separated

350ml double cream

250g tub of mascarpone cheese

50g caster sugar

175g sponge fingers (about 18)

75g pistachio slivers (or whole nuts), finely blitzed in a food processor

Place the white chocolate in a heatproof bowl set over a pan of barely simmering water, without the base of the bowl touching the water, and leave to melt, then remove the bowl and set aside.

Put half the raspberries, the icing sugar and cold water into a food processor or blender and blitz until puréed.

Whisk the egg whites in a small bowl with an electric hand whisk until they form stiff peaks. In a separate bowl, whip the cream to soft peaks.

Put the egg yolks, mascarpone and caster sugar into a large mixing bowl and beat together. Mix in the melted white chocolate, then add the whipped cream a little at a time, gently folding it in with a spatula to keep the mixture light. Once all the cream has been incorporated, add the whisked egg whites a little at a time, again folding them in gently rather than stirring.

Select your serving dish – I use a 26 x 18cm rectangular dish. Use as many sponge fingers as necessary to cover the base of the dish in a single layer, breaking some up if you need to fit them into corners or sides. Pour over the raspberry sauce and spread it out with the back of a spoon so that the sponge finger base is entirely covered, then add the whole raspberries in an even layer. Finally, pour over the white chocolate mixture and shake the dish to allow the mixture to fill any gaps, then smooth over the surface with a spatula. Sprinkle an even layer of the pistachios on top and refrigerate for a minimum of 8 hours or overnight before serving.

Turmeric, orange & coconut rice pudding

Turmeric is an ingredient you need to be incredibly careful with when using in non-savoury recipes, especially the fresh variety – add too much and everything tends to taste like curry. This delicate pudding features the aromatic perfume of turmeric without the harsh back-bite in an orange-scented coconut milk rice, making the perfect combination for a satisfyingly creamy sweet treat. Persians don't generally eat rice pudding as a dessert but as more of a snack in the afternoon or at breakfast. However you enjoy it, this is a unique recipe and definitely one to try, but just make sure you stick to the prescribed quantity of fresh turmeric!

SERVES 6

600ml milk, or more if needed

400g can coconut milk

finely grated zest and juice of
    2 unwaxed oranges

4 tablespoons golden caster sugar

6g fresh turmeric, scrubbed and
    finely grated

1 teaspoon vanilla bean paste

200g short-grain rice

2 handfuls of desiccated coconut,
    plus extra to decorate

Pour the milk and coconut milk into a large saucepan and stir in the orange juice, sugar, turmeric and vanilla. Heat gently over a medium-low heat, without boiling.

Add the rice and cook for about 25 minutes, stirring regularly to draw the starch out of the rice, until tender. If your rice pudding has thickened too much, simply add more milk, or cook for a few more minutes if it needs longer to soften.

When the rice is cooked, stir through the desiccated coconut and orange zest. Serve sprinkled with extra coconut to decorate.

Cheddar & za'atar rolls

I do love cheesy bread – it's one of life's little joys, in my humble opinion. These rolls make wonderful sandwiches as well as being a great alternative to the traditional dinner roll. Do yourself a favour and make a double batch because, if I'm honest, every time I make any sort of bread, I end up eating a hefty portion of it straight from the oven, and if you have to share them, you may just need more than six.

MAKES 6

7g sachet fast-action dried yeast

50ml milk, warmed

500g strong bread flour

200ml lukewarm water

50ml olive oil, plus extra for rubbing

1 teaspoon sea salt flakes

3 heaped tablespoons za'atar

100g vegetarian Cheddar cheese, grated

Add the yeast to the warm (but not hot) milk and stir with a fork until dissolved, then leave the mixture to sit for 5 minutes.

Tip the flour into a mixing bowl and make a well in the centre. Pour the yeast mixture into the well and use a fork to mix into the flour as best as you can. Add the lukewarm water, olive oil and salt, then use your hands to mix together to form a dough. Cover the bowl with clingfilm and leave to rest for 10 minutes, then knead the dough in the bowl for 1 minute. Repeat the resting and kneading process twice more.

Line your largest baking tray with baking paper. Divide the dough into 6 balls on the lined tray, then rub with olive oil. Sprinkle each ball with 1 teaspoon za'atar and rub all over the dough, then sprinkle over a little more za'atar to evenly coat. Scatter an equal quantity of the cheese on top of each roll and sprinkle over the remaining za'atar. Leave to rest in a warm place for 10 minutes.

Meanwhile, preheat the oven to 220°C (200°C fan), Gas Mark 7.

Bake the rolls for 30 minutes until cooked through and the cheese turns golden. Remove from the oven and leave to cool before serving.

Coriander & feta spiced loaf

You can make many wonderful breads without a bread maker. I'm not the most skilled baker by any stretch of the imagination, but this loaf never fails and is really appealing, preferably served still warm and with a generous smear of salted butter.

MAKES 1 LOAF

50g fresh coriander, roughly chopped

120ml olive oil

7g sachet fast-action dried yeast

50ml milk, warmed

500g strong bread flour, plus extra
for dusting if needed

2 teaspoons coriander seeds, toasted
and crushed (see Tip on page 15)

2 teaspoons cumin seeds, toasted
and crushed (see Tip on page 15)

150ml warm water

200g vegetarian feta cheese

Maldon sea salt flakes and freshly
ground black pepper

Put the fresh coriander, stalks and all, into a mini food processor with half the olive oil and 1 tablespoon of warm water and blitz until you have a smooth herb oil.

Add the yeast to the warm (not hot) milk and stir until dissolved, then leave to sit for 5 minutes.

Tip the flour into a mixing bowl, then season generously with pepper and a good amount of salt and mix in. Make a well in the centre, pour the yeast mixture into the well and use a fork to mix into the flour as best as you can. Add the herb oil, toasted crushed seeds, remaining 60ml olive oil and the warm water, then use your hands to mix together to form a dough.

Knead the dough in the bowl for 1 minute and leave to rest for 10 minutes, then repeat the kneading and resting process. Knead again for 1 minute, then add large chunks of the feta to the dough, working it in by stretching the dough over the cheese to envelop it. Shape the dough into a round, dusting with flour if it seems sticky. Transfer to a sheet of baking paper, then place in a large cast-iron pot or on a baking sheet. Cover with a clean tea towel and leave to rise in a warm place for 1 hour.

Preheat the oven to 200°C (180°C fan), Gas Mark 6.

Using a sharp knife, slice a cross in the top of the dough, then bake for 35–40 minutes until cooked through and browned on top – the base should sound hollow when tapped. Leave to cool on a wire rack before serving.

TIP
Using a cast-iron pot will help to cook the loaf from the base.

Index

Author's acknowledgements

To my long-suffering agent Martine Carter, who has to wrangle with me constantly, but who does so with such grace and experience, and always has my best interests at heart – you know how much I appreciate and value you and there is no one better to help me do what I do. Thank you for always keeping me on the straight and narrow and caring beyond what an agent usually would; you are very much like family to me.

To my brilliant publisher and friend Stephanie Jackson at Octopus Publishing, thank you for continuing to support my ideas and working with me to create brilliant books. To the lovely Caroline Brown, Publicity Director at Octopus Publishing, and to your absolutely fantastic team who are the best in the business and work so hard on every new book; without you, Megan and Matt my books wouldn't be as well-known as they are today – you guys always knock it out of the park for me.

To my dear friend, my wonderful, brilliant photographer Kris Kirkham, you are the Zen guru of our shoots. Always funny and supportive, you get me and my food and make working with you and the entire team nothing but pure joy – thank you for yet another beautiful collection of photographs that bring my food to life on every page. And thank you to Kris's assistant, Eyder Rosso Goncalves, for his endless care and kindness on shoots, and to knowing when a recipe is extra successful because you eat it all.

An extra special thank you to my superstar editor Sybella Stephens, who has the incredibly hard task of making my recipe text make sense! Five books in and you make it look easy, but I know it's far from that.

To Jonathan Christie, Jazzy 'Fizzle' Bahra and Peter Hunt for designing and creating yet another beautiful book despite how hard it becomes each time. You have my utmost sympathy for having to work with me, but thank you for your patience and for allowing me to participate in the process.

The most unsung heroes on my photoshoots are the team who make my food look incredible and appealing on every page, so a huge thank you to my food stylist, the incredibly gifted and super-patient Laura Field, for always delivering the perfect plate of food, and to her brilliant (and also very tolerant and patient) assistants Hilary Lester, Sonali Shah and Lizzie Evans.

I wouldn't be anywhere without the tireless efforts of the brilliant Kevin Hawkins; thank you for all your wisdom, experience and opinions that help guide what I do and have always been completely invaluable to me. A big debt of gratitude also to Alison Goff and Denise Bates at Octopus Publishing, for always being incredibly supportive and kind, and making me feel so valued. And to the entire Octopus team, those who I know and may not know, for working all the cogs that make up the bigger picture of our successes together – I am so grateful for all that you've done and continue to do for me every day.

And last, but by no means least, to my mother, Mama Ghayour… who now seems to have her own fan base across social media, who will always be blunt when critiquing my recipes and who still refuses to even try to cook, but who is the best friend, sister, father, mother, travel-partner and official PA any girl could ever ask for. You are the Thelma to my Louise and we drive each other nuts, but I wouldn't have it any other way, and despite your long list of 'foods you don't like', I absolutely adore and respect you and am so grateful to have you as my Mum.